ROSE | BIBLE BASICS

# Names of God
# & Other Bible Studies

D1570577

HENDRICKSON PUBLISHERS   ROSE PUBLISHING

© 2008, 2009 Bristol Works, Inc.
Rose Publishing, LLC
140 Summit Street
P.O. Box 3473
Peabody, Massachusetts 01961-3473
www.hendricksonrose.com

**Free downloadable study guide** at hendricksonrose.com. Click on "information", click on "Free Study Guide Samples", click on "FREE Rose Bible Basics Study Guides and Worksheets" then click on "Names of God Study Guide".

Includes these Rose Publishing Titles:

Names of God © 2003, 2005 RW Research, Inc.
     Authors: Shawn Vander Lugt, MDiv; Carol R. Witte
Names of Jesus © 2006 RW Research, Inc.
     Author: William Brent Ashby
Names of the Holy Spirit © 2008 Bristol Works, Inc.
     Author: William Brent Ashby
The Trinity © 1999, 2005 RW Research, Inc.
     Contributors: Robert M. Bowman, Jr; Dennis L. Okholm, PhD; Gary M. Burge, PhD;
     Paul Carden; Robert Cubillos; Ron Rhodes, PhD
The Ten Commandments © 2006 RW Research, Inc.
     Contributor: Shawn Vander Lugt, MDiv
Lord's Prayer © 2007 Bristol Works, Inc.
     Contributor: Shawn Vander Lugt, MDiv
Beatitudes © 2008 Bristol Works, Inc.
     Authors: William Brent Ashby; Benjamin Galan, MTS, ThM
Fruit of the Spirit © 2004 RW Research, Inc.
     Contributors: G. Goldsmith; Shawn Vander Lugt, MDiv; Carol R. Witte
Armor of God © 2005 RW Research, Inc.
     Author: Timothy Paul Jones, EdD

Library of Congress Cataloging-in-Publication Data

Names of God and other Bible studies.
     p. cm.
  ISBN 978-1-59636-203-1 (pbk.)
  1. Theology, Doctrinal--Popular works. 2. God--Name--Biblical teaching. 3. Jesus Christ--Name--Biblical teaching. 4. Holy Spirit--Name--Biblical teaching.
  BT77.N36 2008
  231--dc22
                         2008007739

Printed by Brilliant Printers Pvt. Ltd.
Printed in India
January 2020, 10th printing

# Names of God
## and Other Bible Studies

# Contents

Continued
on next
page

# Names of God
## and Other Bible Studies

# Contents

# Names
## of God

21 Names of God

The Meaning of Each Name

Bible References

| Name of God | Meaning | Application |
|---|---|---|
| ADONAI | The Lord<br>My Great Lord | God is the Master and majestic Lord. God is our total authority. |
| EL | The Strong One | He is more powerful than any false god. God will overcome all obstacles. We can depend on God. |
| EL ELOHE YISRAEL | God, the God of Israel | The God of Israel is distinct and separate from all false gods of the world. |
| EL ELYON | The God Most High | He is the Sovereign God in whom we can put our trust. El Elyon has supremacy over all false gods. |
| ELOHIM | The All-Powerful One<br>Creator | God is the all-powerful creator of the universe. God knows all, creates all, and is everywhere at all times. The plural of "El." |
| EL OLAM | The Eternal God<br>The Everlasting God | He is the Beginning and the End, the One who works His purposes throughout the ages. He gives strength to the weary. |
| EL ROI | The God Who Sees Me | There are no circumstances in our lives that escape His fatherly awareness and care. God knows us and our troubles. |
| EL SHADDAI | The All Sufficient One,<br>The God of the Mountains,<br>God Almighty | God is the all-sufficient source of all of our blessings. God is all-powerful. Our problems are not too big for God to handle. |
| IMMANUEL | God With Us<br>"I AM" | Jesus is God in our midst. In Him all the fullness of Deity dwells in bodily form. |
| JEHOVAH<br>(YHWH, SEE COMMENTS P. 9) | "I AM," The One Who Is<br>The Self-Existent One | God never changes. His promises never fail. When we are faithless, He is faithful. We need to obey Him. |
| JEHOVAH-JIREH | The Lord Will Provide | Just as God provided a ram as a substitute for Isaac, He provided His son Jesus as the ultimate sacrifice. God will meet all our needs. |

| References | Comments |
|---|---|
| Psalm 8; Isaiah 40:3-5; Ezekiel 16:8; Habakkuk 3:19 | **Pronounced: ah-doe-NI** *Adonai* (plural) is derived from the singular *Adon* (Lord). This term was pronounced in substitution of *YHWH* (considered too sacred to be uttered). |
| Exodus 15:2; Numbers 23:22; Deuteronomy 7:9 (Mark 15:34) | **Pronounced: el** Occurs more than 200 times in the Old Testament (including compounds). Generic Semitic name for God, used by other cultures to refer to their gods. *El* is used in compound proper names such as Isra-*el* (wrestles with God), Beth-*el* (House of God), and *El*-isha (God is salvation). |
| Genesis 33:20; Exodus 5:1; Psalm 68:8; Psalm 106:48 | **Pronounced: el el-o-HAY yis-raw-ALE** The name of the altar that Jacob (Israel) erected after his encounter with God and God's blessing upon him. (Genesis 32:24-30; 33:19, 20) |
| Genesis 14:17-22; Psalm 78:35; Daniel 4:34 (Acts 16:17) | **Pronounced: el EL-yuhn** Melchizedek, the king of Salem (Jeru "Salem") and the priest of God Most High, referred to God as "El Elyon" three times when he blessed Abram. |
| Genesis 1:1-3; Deuteronomy 10:17; Psalm 68 (Mark 13:19) | **Pronounced: el-o-HEEM** Plural form of *El*. This name is usually associated with God in relation to His creation. Some people use the plural word "Elohim" as proof for the Trinity. (Genesis 1:26) *Elohim* is also used to refer to false gods and even human judges. (Psalm 82:6, 7; John 10:34) |
| Genesis 21:33; Psalm 90:1, 2; Isaiah 40:28 (Romans 1:20) | **Pronounced: el o-LAHM** Jesus Christ possesses eternal attributes. He is the same yesterday and today and forever. (Hebrews 13:8) He obtained eternal redemption for us. (Hebrews 9:12) |
| Genesis 16:11-14; Psalm 139:7-12 | **Pronounced: el ROY** Hagar called the Lord by this name beside a fountain of water in the wilderness. God knows all of our thoughts and feelings. Jesus knew the thoughts of those around him, demonstrating that he is *El Roi*. (Matthew 22:18; 26:21, 34; Luke 5:21-24) |
| Genesis 17:1-3; 35:11; 48:3; 49:25; Psalm 90:2 | **Pronounced: el-shaw-DIE** Some scholars suggest that *Shaddai* refers to God's power evident in His judgment. Others suggest that *El Shaddai* means "God of the Mountains." God refers to Himself as "El Shaddai" when he confirms his covenant with Abraham. |
| Isaiah 7:14; 8:8-10 (Matthew 1:23) | **Pronounced: ih-MAN-u-el** This name indicates that Jesus is more than man. He is also God. Isaiah said that the child born to the virgin would be called "Immanuel." (Isaiah 7:14; 9:6) He is the radiance of God's glory and the exact representation of His nature. (Hebrews 1:3) |
| Exodus 3:14; 6:2-4; 34:5-7; Psalm 102 | **Pronounced: juh-HO-vah** A 16th century German translator wrote the name *YHVH* (*YHWH*) using the vowels of *Adonai*, because the ancient Jewish texts from which he was translating had the vowels of *Adonai* under the consonants of *YHVH*. By doing this, he incorrectly came up with the name *Jehovah* (*YaHoVaH*.) |
| Genesis 22:13, 14; Psalm 23 (Mark 10:45; Romans 8:2) | **Pronounced: juh-HO-vah JI-rah** Also known as YHWH-Jireh. Abraham called the place "The Lord will provide" where God provided a ram to be sacrificed instead of his son Isaac. Jesus said that He was the bread of life and anyone who comes to Him will be provided for. (John 6:35) |

| Name of God | Meaning | Application |
|---|---|---|
| JEHOVAH-MEKADDISHKEM | The Lord Who Sanctifies | God sets us apart as a chosen people, a royal priesthood, holy unto God, a people of His own. He cleanses our sin and helps us mature. |
| JEHOVAH-NISSI | The Lord is My Banner | God gives us victory against the flesh, the world and the devil. Our battles are His battles of light against darkness, and good against evil. |
| JEHOVAH-RAPHA | The Lord Who Heals | God has provided the final cure for spiritual, physical, and emotional sickness in Jesus Christ. God can heal us. |
| JEHOVAH-ROHI | The Lord is My Shepherd | The Lord protects, provides, directs, leads, and cares for His people. God tenderly takes care of us as a strong and patient shepherd. |
| JEHOVAH-SABAOTH | The Lord of Hosts<br>The Lord of Armies | The Lord of the hosts of heaven will always fulfill His purposes, even when the hosts of His earthly people fail. |
| JEHOVAH-SHALOM | The Lord is Peace | God defeats our enemies to bring us peace. Jesus is our Prince of Peace. God brings inner peace and harmony. |
| JEHOVAH-SHAMMAH | The Lord is There<br>The Lord My Companion | God's presence is not limited or contained in the Tabernacle or Temple, but is accessible to all who love and obey Him. |
| JEHOVAH-TSIDKENU | The Lord Our Righteousness | Jesus is the King who would come from David's line, and is the one who imparts His righteousness to us. |
| YAH, OR JAH | "I AM," The One Who Is The Self-Existent One | God never changes. His promises never fail. When we are faithless, He is faithful. God promises His continuing presence. |
| YHWH | "I AM," The One Who Is The Self-Existent One | God never changes. His promises never fail. When we are faithless, He is faithful. |

| References | Comments |
|---|---|
| Exodus 31:12, 13 (1 Peter 1:15, 16; Hebrews 13:12; 1 Thessalonians 5:23, 24) | **Pronounced: juh-HO-vah mek-KAH-dish-KIM** Also known as YHWH-Mekaddishkem. We have been set apart, made holy, and redeemed by the blood of Jesus Christ, our *Jehovah-Mekaddishkem*. Therefore, we are to continue to live our lives holy and pleasing to God. (1 Peter 1:13-25) |
| Exodus 17:15, 16; Deuteronomy 20:3, 4; Isaiah 11:10-12 (Ephesians 6:10-18) | **Pronounced: juh-HO-vah NEE-see** Also known as YHWH-Nissi. Name of the altar built by Moses after defeating the Amalekites at Rephidim. Isaiah prophesies that the "Root of Jesse" (Jesus) will stand as a banner for the peoples. (Isaiah 11:10) |
| Exodus 15:25-27; Psalm 103:3; 147:3 (1 Peter 2:24) | **Pronounced: juh-HO-vah RAH-fah** Also known as *YHWH-Rapha*. Jesus demonstrated that He was *Jehovah-Rapha* in his healing of the sick, blind, lame, and casting out demons. Jesus also heals His people from sin and unrighteousness. (Luke 5:31, 32) |
| Psalm 23:1-3; Isaiah 53:6 (John 10:14-18; Hebrews 13:20; Revelation 7:17) | **Pronounced: juh-HO-vah RO-hee** Also known as *YHWH-Ra'ah* (RAH-ah). Jesus is the good shepherd who laid down His life for all people. |
| 1 Samuel 1:3; 17:45; Psalm 46:7; Malachi 1:10-14 (Romans 9:29) | **Pronounced: juh-HO-vah sah-bah-OATH** Also known as *YHWH-Sabaoth*. Many English versions of the Bible translate *Sabaoth* as Almighty. "Jehovah-Sabaoth" is often translated as *The Lord Almighty*. Sabaoth is also translated as *Heavenly Hosts* or *Armies*. |
| Numbers 6:22-27; Judges 6:22-24; Isaiah 9:6 (Hebrews 13:20) | **Pronounced: juh-HO-vah shah-LOME** Also known as *YHWH-Shalom*. Name of the altar built by Gideon at Ophrah to memorialize God's message "Peace be unto thee." Isaiah tells us that the Messiah will also be known as the "Prince of Peace," our Jehovah-Shalom. (Isaiah 9:6) |
| Ezekiel 48:35; Psalm 46 (Matthew 28:20; Revelation 21) | **Pronounced: juh-HO-vah SHAHM-mah** Also known as *YHWH-Shammah*. God revealed to Ezekiel that the name of the New Jerusalem shall be "The Lord is there." Through Jesus Christ, the Spirit of God dwells in us. (1 Corinthians 3:16) |
| Jeremiah 23:5, 6; 33:16; Ezekiel 36:26, 27 (2 Corinthians 5:21) | **Pronounced: juh-HO-vah tsid-KAY-noo** Also known as *YHWH-Tsidkenu*. All people sin and fall short of God's glory, but God freely makes us righteous through faith in Jesus Christ. (Romans 3:22, 23) God promised to send a King who will reign wisely and do what is just and right. The people will live in safety. (Jeremiah 23:5, 6) |
| Exodus 3:14; 15:2; Psalm 46:1; 68:4; Isaiah 26:4 | **Pronounced: Yah** Shorter form of *Yahweh*. It is often used when combined with other names or phrases. Hallelujah means "Praise Yah (the Lord)," Elijah means "God is Yah (the Lord)," and Joshua means "Yah (the Lord) is my salvation." |
| Exodus 3:14; Malachi 3:6 | **Pronounced: YAH-way** God's personal name given to Moses. Also called the tetragrammaton ("four letters"). Occurs about 6,800 times. Translated "LORD" in English versions of the Bible, because it became common practice for Jews to say "Lord" (Adonai) instead of saying the name *YHWH*. |

# Jesus is:

**God:** In the beginning was the Word, and the Word was with God, and the Word was God. ... (John 1:1)

**One with God:** "I and my Father are one." (John 10:30)

**Eternal:** And he laid his right hand upon me, saying unto me, "Fear not; I am the First and the Last." (Revelation 1:17b)

**Omnipresent:** Omnipresent means present everywhere. And [God] hath put all things under his feet, and gave him to be the head over all things to the church, which is his body, the fullness of him that filleth all in all. (Ephesians 1:22, 23)

**Omniscient:** Omniscient means all-knowing. "Lord, thou knowest all things...." (John 21:17)

**Life giving:** In him was life; and the life was the light of men. (John 1:4)

Often in the Scriptures Jesus is called, or compared to, God's names found in the Old Testament. Jesus would allude to his divine nature by comparing Himself to several names used for God. Here are a few examples of Jesus being compared to God:

**El Olam:** The Beginning and the End: "I am Alpha and Omega, the beginning and the end, the first and the last." (Revelation 22:13)

**Jehovah-Jireh:** The Lord will Provide: "I am the bread of life. He that cometh to me shall never hunger, and he that believeth on me shall never thirst." (John 6:35)

**YHWH-Rohi:** The Lord is my Shepherd: "I am the good shepherd: the good shepherd giveth his life for the sheep." (John 10:11)

**YHWH-Tsidkenu:** The Lord is Righteousness: For he hath made him to be sin for us, who knew no sin; that we might be made the righteousness of God in him. (2 Corinthians 5:21)

**YHWH-Rapha:** The Lord Who Heals: Who his own self bare our sins in his own body on the tree, that we, being dead to sins, should live unto righteousness: by whose stripes ye were healed. (1 Peter 2:24)

**El Shaddai:** The All Sufficient One: "My grace is sufficient for thee: for my strength is made perfect in weakness..." (2 Corinthians 12:9)

**Immanuel:** God With Us: ...they shall call his name Emmanuel, which being interpreted is, God with us. (Matthew 1:23)

**YHWH-Shalom:** The Lord is Peace: "Peace I leave with you; my peace I give unto you...." (John 14:27)

# Personal Reflection

## Did you know that...?

• The first name mentioned in the Bible is the fourth word, GOD (Genesis 1:1).

• The name of God in Genesis 1:1 is Elohim.

• Elohim is found over 2,300 times in the Bible referring to God.

• In Psalm 68, Elohim is used 26 times.

• The three most basic names of God are El, Elohim, and Yahweh (Jehovah).

• In Deuteronomy 5:9, all three names are used. "I the LORD (Yahweh) thy God (Elohim)

  am a jealous God (El)..."

• God wants a relationship with us. See Genesis 17:1-8 and Psalm 91.

## Jehovah-Sabaoth

Throughout Scripture, God's people would call on Jehovah-Sabaoth in times of despair. Some examples occur in 1 Samuel. Read the following passages and see how the Lord of Hosts (Armies) helped Hannah and David in their time of great distress and need.

— 1 Samuel 1:1-20
— 1 Samuel 17:41-47

At times, things seem so overwhelming that we find ourselves in complete despair. Despair can be caused by financial, emotional, spiritual, or physical hardships. The Bible promises us that if we approach God with a righteous heart (Proverbs 18:10), He will deliver us from out of the midst of our troubles, just like He delivered Hannah and David. On a sheet of paper, or in your personal journal, spend several minutes reflecting and journaling on those times when Jehovah-Sabaoth delivered you from trouble and call on Him for help in your current need.

# Amazing Verses
# about The Lord of Hosts

| | |
|---|---|
| Genesis 2:1 | Daniel 4:35 |
| Psalm 148:1, 2 | Nehemiah 9:6 |
| I Kings 22:19 | Psalm 68:17 |
| Matthew 25:31 | Matthew 26:53 |

What do these verses tell you about God?
Pray that Jesus will open your mind to understand the Scriptures. (Luke 24:45)

# Psalm 23 and Names of God

Reflect on how Psalm 23 refers to God who is always with you.

| | |
|---|---|
| Verse 1: | The LORD is my shepherd—Jehovah-Rohi |
| | I shall not want—Jehovah-Jireh |
| Verse 2: | He maketh me to lie down in green pastures. He leadeth me beside |
| | the still waters—Jehovah-Shalom |
| Verse 3: | He restoreth my soul—Jehovah-Rapha |
| | He leadeth me in the paths of righteousness for His name's sake |
| | —Jehovah-Tsidkenu |
| Verse 5: | Thou anointest my head with oil—Jehovah-Mekaddishkem |

## Have You Heard?

*Hast thou not known? hast thou not heard,*
*that the everlasting God, the LORD,*
*the Creator of the ends of the earth,*
*fainteth not, neither is weary?*
*There is no searching of his understanding.*
*He giveth power to the faint;*
*and to them that have no might he increaseth strength...*
*But they that wait upon the LORD shall renew their strength;*
*they shall mount up with wings as eagles;*
*they shall run, and not be weary;*
*and they shall walk, and not faint.*
(Isaiah 40:28, 29, 31)

## Worship God

Choose one of the names of Jesus. What does it mean to you personally?
Write a prayer or song of worship and honor to God using one of His names.

Scripture taken from the HOLY BIBLE: KING JAMES VERSION
Authors: Shawn Vander Lugt, MDiv; Carol R. Witte

# Names
# of Jesus

50 Names of Jesus

The Meaning of Each Name

Bible References

| Name | References | Meaning |
|------|-----------|---------|
| ALMIGHTY | Revelation 1:8 | Jesus is all-powerful. |
| AUTHOR AND FINISHER | Hebrews 12:2 | Jesus is our start and finish. |
| BELOVED | Ephesians 1:6 | Jesus is at the center of God's love. |
| BRANCH | Isaiah 11:1; Jeremiah 23:5; Zechariah 3:8; 6:12 | Jesus is the shoot from David's line. |
| BREAD OF LIFE | John 6:32-35 | Jesus is our sustenance. |
| BRIDEGROOM | Matthew 9:15; John 3:29; Rev. 21:9 | Jesus leads and cares for us. |
| BRIGHT MORNING STAR | Revelation 22:16 | Jesus lights our way. |
| CARPENTER | Mark 6:3 | Jesus is one of us. |
| CHOSEN ONE | Luke 23:35 | Jesus is God's Chosen One. |
| CHIEF CORNERSTONE | Isaiah 28:16; Psalm 118:22; Ephesians 2:20; 1 Peter 2:6 | Jesus is our rock of safety. |
| DOOR | John 10:9 | Jesus is our gateway. |
| EMMANUEL/ IMMANUEL | Isaiah 7:14 – 8:8; Matthew 1:23 | Jesus is God with us. |

| Insights | Related Titles (by root word and/or theme) |
|---|---|
| Christ is the All-Powerful Lord. Nothing is beyond His reach or impossible for Him. | Mighty God, Mighty in Battle, Potentate, Power of God (Isaiah 9:6; Psalm 24:8; 1 Timothy 6:15; 1 Corinthians 1:24) |
| Jesus was at the beginning of creation and will be there to the end. He is both the author of all that is and the one who sees His creation through to the end. | Alpha and Omega, Beginning and End, First and Last (Revelation 1:8; 21:6; 22:13) |
| Christ is the Beloved Son of the Father, and as such, the desire of all people who love God. All who love God will be drawn to Jesus. | Desire of all nations (Haggai 2:7) Associate of God (Zechariah 13:7) |
| Jesus is the offshoot of the line of David and paradoxically also the root. He is the vine on which we depend for life and nourishment. | Nazarene (Netzer = Branch in Hebrew; Matthew 2:23; Isaiah 11:1) Root of David, Shoot, Vine (Revelation 5:5; Isaiah 11:10; 53:2; John 15:1) |
| Jesus was born in Bethlehem, which means "the house of bread." He is our spiritual nourishment and the sustenance of the world. All things are kept alive by Him. | Living Bread (John 6:5) Living Water (John 7:37, 38) |
| Jesus is the bridegroom and His church is the bride. He is the head of the church and cares for her. | Head of the Church (Ephesians 5:23) Head of the Body (Ephesians 4:15, 16) |
| Jesus is the brightest star in the heavens and the Light of the World. We shall not lose our way in His light. | Day Star (2 Peter 1:19) Star (Numbers 24:17) Sunrise (Luke 1:78) Sun of Righteousness (Malachi 4:2) |
| Jesus, the creator of wood, became a worker of wood, and died on a cross of wood for us (Galatians 3:13). | Carpenter's Son (Matthew 13:55) |
| Jesus is God's Chosen One, chosen for glory and great sacrifice. We, in Him, are God's chosen people. | Elect One (Isaiah 42:1) |
| Jesus is the cornerstone which the religious leaders rejected, but which God chose from eternity to build His house, a temple of living stone! We can rely on Him as our solid foundation. | Foundation, Living Stone, Precious Stone, Rock, Rock of Offense, Stone (1 Corinthians 3:11; 1 Peter 2:4; Isaiah 28:16; 1 Corinthians 10:4; 1 Peter 2:8; Psalm 118:22) |
| Jesus is our opening to God. He is the only way to heaven. | Door of the Sheepfold (John 10:7) See Way. |
| Jesus was born on earth as a real human being. He entered space and time to become one of us so we might be with God forever. | Only Begotten God (John 1:18) |

| Name | References | Meaning |
|------|-----------|---------|
| ETERNAL FATHER | Isaiah 9:6; 1 John 1:1-3 | Jesus is forever. |
| FAITHFUL AND TRUE WITNESS | Revelation 1:5; 3:14 | Jesus is faithful. |
| FIRSTBORN | Hebrews 12:23; Revelation 5 | Jesus is our elder brother. |
| GOD | John 1:1, 14-18; Romans 9:5; Titus 2:13; Heb. 1:8 | Jesus is God. |
| HEAD OF THE CHURCH | Ephesians 5:23 | Jesus leads the church. |
| HIGH PRIEST, APOSTLE | Hebrews 3:1, 2 | Jesus is our prophet and priest. |
| HOLY ONE | Mark 1:24; Acts 2:27; 3:14; Psalm 16:10 | Jesus is perfect. |
| HOPE | 1 Timothy 1:1 | Jesus is our confidence. |
| IMAGE OF THE INVISIBLE GOD | 2 Corinthians 4:4; Colossians 1:15 | Jesus is the perfect picture of God. |
| JESUS | Matthew 1:21 | Jesus saves. |
| JUDGE/RULER | John 5:22, 23; Micah 4:3; Matthew 26:67; Acts 10:42 | Jesus is our judge as well as our advocate and lawyer. |

| Insights | Related Titles (by root word and/or theme) |
|---|---|
| Christ had no beginning and has no end. He is the source of time, space, and all creation. | Head of the Creation of God (Revelation 3:14) |
| Christ is Truth in the flesh. His witness is always faithful. We can trust His word. | Amen (Revelation 3:14) Faithful and True (Revelation 19:11) Truth (John 14:6) |
| Christ is the firstborn of the dead, the firstfruits of a new humanity, resurrected in new form. As our eldest brother (Hebrews 2:11), He is heir of all things. (The importance of the firstborn is also connected to Passover. At the Exodus, the firstborn child of the Hebrews was "passed over." He was saved from death by the sacrifice of a lamb.) | Firstfruits (1 Corinthians 15:20) Firstborn from the Dead (Colossians 1:18) |
| Christ is in His very nature God and all the fullness of that essence is in Him. He is worthy of our worship. | Fullness of God (Colossians 2:9) See *Son of God* and *Yahweh*. |
| Jesus is the leader and Lord of the church. True believers will follow Him as He cares for them and directs their way. | Head of the Body (Ephesians 4:15, 16) See *Bridegroom*. |
| An apostle is someone who has directly communicated with God and is authorized to speak for him. A high priest is God's appointed person to represent the people to Himself. Jesus is both God's spokesman and our representative to God. | Bishop of Souls, Minister of the Sanctuary, the Prophet (1 Peter 2:25; Hebrews 8:1-2; Deuteronomy 18:15, 18; John 6:14) |
| Christ is without sin and evil. Because of this, He became the only perfect man to walk upon the earth. Therefore, He is the only one who could die to save us. | Holy Child, Lord Our Righteousness, Righteous One, Sanctification (Acts 4:30, Jeremiah 23:5, 6; 1 John 2:1; 1 Corinthians 1:30) |
| Jesus is our only source of hope in the world. His conquest of death gives us confidence now and for the future. | Hope of Glory (Colossians 1:27) Hope of Israel (Jeremiah 17:13) |
| Because Christ and the Father are one in nature, Jesus perfectly reflects God. When we look at Him, we see what God looks like as a man. | Exact Representation of His Nature (Hebrews 1:3) |
| Jesus is the Greek form of the Hebrew *Yeshua* (Joshua). The name means "Yahweh (Jehovah) is salvation." | Yeshua (Joshua) |
| Jesus, the very one who is our Advocate before the bar of God's justice, has been made the Judge of all. (Romans 8:33, 34) | See *Wonderful Counselor*. |

| Name | References | Meaning |
|------|-----------|---------|
| KING OF KINGS | Revelation 17:14 | Jesus is king over all. |
| LAMB OF GOD | John 1:29, 36; 1 Peter 1:19; Rev. 5:6-12; 7:17 | Jesus is our sacrifice. |
| LAST ADAM | 1 Corinthians 15:45 | Jesus is the Father of a new human nature. |
| LIGHT OF THE WORLD | John 8:12 | Jesus is the light. |
| LION OF THE TRIBE OF JUDAH | Genesis 49:9, 10; Revelation 5:5 | Jesus is David's son. |
| LIVING WATER SPIRIT | John 4:10; 7:38 | Jesus is our spiritual drink. |
| LORD OF LORDS | Revelation 19:16; 1 Timothy 6:15 | Jesus is Lord. |
| MAN OF SORROWS | Isaiah 53:3 | Jesus bore our sorrows. |
| MASTER | Matthew 8:19 | Jesus is our teacher. |
| MESSENGER OF THE COVENANT | Malachi 3:1 | Jesus is God's final messenger. |
| MESSIAH | Daniel 9:25; John 1:41; 4:25 | Jesus is Messiah. |

| Insights | Related Titles (by root word and/or theme) |
|---|---|
| Christ is the king over all kings and rulers. As subjects in His kingdom, we owe Him our complete allegiance. | King, King of Israel, King of the Jews, Lord of Lords, Master, Prince, Ruler Sovereign (Matt. 21:5; Jn. 1:49; Matt. 2:2; Rev. 19:16; Lk. 8:24; Dan. 9:25; 1 Tim. 6:15) |
| Jesus is the fulfillment of the whole sacrificial system (Hebrews 7:26-29), especially as our Passover Lamb. As the Lamb of God, Jesus' sacrifice pays for our sins past, present, and future. | Offering (Hebrews 10:10) Passover (1 Corinthians 5:7) Propitiation (1 John 2:2) Sacrifice (Ephesians 5:2) |
| The first Adam brought sin and death. Jesus is the Last Adam, bringing life. From Him flows eternal life. | Man, Second Man, Son of Man (Daniel 7:13-14; Mark 9:31; John 19:5; 1 Timothy 2:5) |
| Jesus' radiance reveals God. Knowing Jesus is to know and see what God is like. Those who follow Him will not walk in darkness (John 8:12). | Light, Radiance of God's Glory (John 1:4, 5; Hebrews 1:3) See *Bright Morning Star.* |
| Jesus fulfills the Old Testament prophecies, being from the tribe of Judah and the lineage of David. | Son of David (Matthew 12:23) See *King of Kings.* |
| Christ is the fountainhead of the life that wells up inside every believer like an unending spring. | Fountain Life-Giving Spirit (Jeremiah 2:13; Zechariah 13:1; 1 Cor. 15:45) |
| Jesus is Lord over all! He has this title by right as the Son of God and Creator of the cosmos. It is also a title He has earned by His humble work of becoming human in order to redeem us through His death. | Lord (Philippians 2:11) See *King of Kings.* |
| Jesus did not come to enjoy a life of happy kingship over the world. He came to carry the world's sins and sorrows, that we might have eternal joy with Him and God the Father. | Servant, Slave (Isaiah 42:1, 2; 49:7; 52:13–53:12; Matthew 12:18-20) |
| *Master* means "teacher" or "rabbi." Jesus is the final source of truth concerning God. He is the only teacher who can show us the way to go. | Rabbi, Rabboni, Teacher, Truth (John 20:16; John 14:6, 7) |
| *Messenger* and *angel* are the same word in both the Old and New Testaments. Christ is God's ultimate messenger of the New Covenant of God's grace and head of God's angelic armies. | Angel of the Lord, Captain of the Lord's Host (Exodus 3:2; Judges 13:15-18; Joshua 5:14) |
| *Messiah* is the Hebrew word, translated into Greek, as *Christ.* Both words mean "Anointed One" (one especially appointed by God for His plan and purpose). | Christ, Anointed One (Matthew 1:16; Psalm 2:1, 2) |

| Name | References | Meaning |
| --- | --- | --- |
| PRINCE OF PEACE | Isaiah 9:6 | Jesus is our peace. |
| PROPHET | John 6:14; 7:40; Deuteronomy 18:15-22; Luke 7:16; Matthew 21:11 | Jesus is the prophet foretold. |
| REDEEMER | Job 19:25 | Jesus is our redemption. |
| RESURRECTION AND THE LIFE | John 11:25 | Jesus is life. |
| SAVIOR | Luke 1:47-2:11; John 4:42; 1 John 4:14 | Jesus is our salvation. |
| SHEPHERD | 1 Peter 2:25 | Jesus is the good shepherd. |
| SHILOH | Genesis 49:10 | Jesus is our promised peace. |
| SON OF GOD | Luke 1:35; Hebrews 4:14 | Jesus is the Son of God by nature. |
| TRUE VINE | John 15:1 | Jesus is our evergreen source of life. |
| THE WAY, THE TRUTH, AND THE LIFE | John 14:6; Acts 9:2 | Jesus is our path to God. |

## Insights

## Related Titles (by root word and/or theme)

Christ is our peace. He has ended the conflict between God and man by His death on the cross. He has also given us internal peace by the love that is planted in our hearts by His Spirit.

Peace (Ephesians 2:14)
King of Salem (Hebrews 7:1, 2)

Long before Jesus was born, Moses and others prophesied that a prophet like him would come speaking God's words. Jesus is that Prophet, the ultimate and final spokesman for God.

See *High Priest.*

Christ's death is the payment that redeems us from the debt we owe to God's law, ransoming our lives and guaranteeing us a place in His family.

Kinsman, Ransom, Redemption, Guarantee (Ruth 2:14; Matthew 20:28; 1 Timothy 2:6; 1 Corinthians 1:30; Hebrews 7:22)

Christ is Life itself. Death could not hold Him, nor can it hold any who are in Him.

Living One (Revelation 1:18)
See *Firstborn.*

Christ is the Savior of the world who came to deliver us from the power of death. He is the one who seeks and saves the lost.

Captain of Salvation, Deliverer, Horn of Salvation, Salvation (Hebrews 2:10; Romans 11:26; Luke 1:69; 2:30)

Jesus came to care for and to lead lost sheep, lost men and women. His sheep know His voice and no one can take them from His hands.

Door of the Sheepfold, Good Shepherd (John 10:7, 14) See *Door.*

*Shiloh* may be translated as "to whom the scepter belongs," or as a name derived from the Hebrew word for peace. Jesus fulfills the prophecy by being the King to whom the scepter belongs and our Prince of Peace.

See *Messiah* and *Prince of Peace.*

Christ is the only "natural" Son of God, which means He partakes in the Divine nature fully. We become God's children by adoption and inherit all creation in, and with, Christ.

Only Begotten, Son of the Most High, Heir (John 1:14, 18; Luke 1:32; Hebrews 1:2) See *God.*

Jesus is our connection to the source of life. As God He has life in Himself. Having become a man He extends that life to all who believe.

See *Branch.*

Jesus is the Way to God. He is the path to truth and life. No mere human teacher, He is the map, the road, the destination and the one who has gone ahead of us.

Forerunner, Jacob's Ladder (Hebrews 6:20; Genesis 28:12; John 1:51)

| Name | References | Meaning |
| --- | --- | --- |
| WISDOM OF GOD | 1 Corinthians 1:24, 30 | Jesus is our wisdom from God. |
| WONDERFUL COUNSELOR | Isaiah 9:6 | Jesus is our defense attorney. |
| WORD | John 1:1, 14 | Jesus is God's Word. |
| YAHWEH (JEHOVAH*) | Isaiah 40:3-5; Matthew 3:3; 28:19; Philippians 2:6-11; Exodus 3:14 | Jesus has God's name. |

| Names of God | Meaning | References |
| --- | --- | --- |
| YAHWEH*-YIREH | God Will Provide | Genesis 22:13, 14 |
| YAHWEH-MEKADDISHKEM | The Lord Who Sanctifies | Exodus 31:12, 13 |
| YAHWEH-NISSI | The Lord is My Banner | Exodus 17:15, 16 |
| YAHWEH-RAPHA | The Lord Who Heals | Exodus 15:25-27 |
| YAHWEH-ROHI | The Lord is My Shepherd | Psalm 23:1-3 |
| YAHWEH-SABAOTH | The Lord of Hosts | 1 Samuel 1:3 |
| YAHWEH-SHALOM | The Lord is Peace | Numbers 6:22-27 |
| YAHWEH-SHAMMAH | The Lord is There | Ezekiel 48:35 |
| YAHWEH-TSIDKANU | The Lord Our Righteousness | Jeremiah 23:5, 6; 33:16 |

*Using the vowels of *Adonai* (Lord) and the consonants of *YHVH* (God), a 16th-century German translator incorrectly translated *YHVH* as *YaHoVah*, resulting in the name *Jehovah*. Yahweh is the more accepted spelling for God's name.

## Insights

Though the reference in Proverbs is not a strict prophetic word about Christ, the concept of wisdom as a person and associate of God is fulfilled in Jesus. To know Jesus is to be connected to the wisdom of the ages.

Christ is our Wonderful Counselor before God. He comforts, consoles and counsels us as our Mediator and Intercessor. As our Advocate before God, He defends us like a lawyer before the bar of God's justice, offering Himself as a payment for our crimes.

Jesus is the speech uttered by God the Father, impelled by the breath of God's Spirit. He is not merely information, but the effective, powerful Word that calls creation out of nothing and life out of death.

The holy name *Yahweh* means "He who is." It expresses the idea that only God has self-existent being. The name was so holy that the Jews would not utter it out loud. Christ possesses this name.

## Related Titles (by root word and/or theme)

*Compare personified wisdom*
(Proverbs 8:22-31; Luke 11:49)

Advocate, Comforter, Consolation of Israel, Daysman, Intercessor, Mediator, Paraclete (1 John 2:1; John 14:16; Luke 2:25; Job 9:33; 1 Timothy 2:5) See *Judge*.

Word of God, Word of Life
(1 John 1:1)

I AM; Who was, Who is and Who is to come (Mark 6:50; Luke 21:8; John 8:24, 28, 58; Revelation 4:8)

## Parallel Verses Referring to Jesus

"I am the bread of life." (John 6:35)

We have been made holy by the blood of Jesus. (Hebrews 13:12)

Jesus, the root of Jesse, is our banner. (Isaiah 11:10)

By His stripes we are healed. (1 Peter 2:24)

"I am the good Shepherd." (John 10:11)

Jesus will come as King of Kings. (Revelation 1:8)

Jesus is the Prince of Peace. (Isaiah 9:6)

Jesus said that He will be present in our hearts. (Matthew 28:20)

Because of Jesus, we are righteous before God. (2 Corinthians 5:21)

# WHAT DOES IT MEAN
# TO PRAY IN JESUS' NAME?

Jesus himself instructed us to do it (John 16:24), but do we understand it? To pray in Jesus' name means to pray in the authority of that name, much as we might use the phrase "in the name of the law" to assert the authority of the law. But the use of Jesus' name should be more than a mere postscript on our prayers, more even than an authoritative letterhead. To pray effectively in Christ's name, we must be "in Him"—in union with his life and death. In his letters, Paul uses the prepositions "in" and "together with" to emphasize the connectedness of the believer to Christ and His authority and power.

Praying in Jesus' name does not give our prayers extra power. The truth is, prayers are completely powerless in the first place unless they are "in Jesus." Without Christ's intercession, no prayers would make it to the ears of God. The reason we are told to pray in and by his authority is not as some magic formula, but to put our own spirits and our own thinking in the right place—under and in him.

**"No" for an Answer**

Of course this means we must be willing to accept "no" as an answer. Even God's "no" is not a "No way," but "No, I have something better in mind." Christ's prayer in Gethsemane before His crucifixion should teach us both about whose authority we are under and about accepting God's better plan (Matthew 26:39; Mark 14:36; Luke 22:42). Christ invites us to pray in his name, assuring us that whatever is asked, by his authority and in faith, will be granted by God. This means that, first, we must be connected to God in Christ, and second, that we must know we have what we ask.

For Christians, the second part is often difficult, even impossible. Christ's Gethsemane prayer ("Let this cup pass from me"), the only request He made that was denied, teaches us that there are some things we ask for—good as they may seem—that are not God's best for us. Jesus knew it was the Father's will that He should suffer on our behalf; many of our prayers may also fall into this category. But observe the powerful results: In Jesus' case, as in ours, the ultimate outcome will be life out of death.

We should think of our prayers as Christ's own prayers through us, inspired and led by the Holy Spirit. God has already planned out the good works we are to walk in; these include our prayers (Ephesians 2:10). Seeing our prayers as Jesus' prayers *through us* should cause us to rethink what we ask for. It should also cause us to think about our union with Christ. Real authority always flows from the author. Are we connected to the Author and Perfecter of our faith?

Author: William Brent Ashby

# Names
## of the
# Holy Spirit

32 Names of the Holy Spirit

The Meaning of Each Name

Bible References

# *The* HOLY SPIRIT

Much controversy and confusion exists in understanding who the Holy Spirit is and what he does.

• Many consider the Spirit to be impersonal, rather like a force—the energy or power of God. The Scriptures confirm the powerful nature of the Holy Spirit. He is named the Power of God and Spirit of Might, and yet the Bible tells us much more about him. Unlike a mere force, he can be lied to (Acts 5:3–4), he can be grieved (Ephesians 4:30), he has a name (Matthew 28:19).

• Other people see the Spirit as the common bond of love among God's people. The Scriptures call him the Spirit of grace, of mercy and of comfort; but he is also called the Spirit of truth and judgment (discernment), indicating that he is more than simply a warm fuzzy feeling we get when we are together.

• Some understand the Holy Spirit as the mind, the intellect, behind creation. To be sure, he is the Spirit of wisdom and understanding, but more than a cosmic computer. He is in fact God, the third Person of the Trinity.

Studying the names of the Spirit found in the Bible will help us get a fuller, well-rounded idea of who he is and how he operates and so allow us to worship and serve God in a fuller and richer capacity.

# *The* TRINITY

In the simplest of terms, Christians believe that there is only one God, and this one God exists as one essence in three Persons—the Father, the Son, and the Holy Spirit.

## Why do Christians Believe in the Trinity?
• The Bible clearly teaches that there is only one God, yet it calls all three Persons God.
• There is only one God (Deuteronomy 6:4; Isaiah 44:6, 8; 45:5a).
• The Father is God (1 Corinthians 8:6; Ephesians 4:4-6).
• The Son is God (John 1:1-5, 14; John 10:30-33; John 20:28; Hebrews 1:6-8; Philippians 2:9-11; see these passages about Jesus' deity: Isaiah 7:14; Isaiah 9:6; John 1:1; John 1:18; John 8:58, 59; John 10:30; Acts 20:28; Romans 9:5 & 10:9-13; Colossians 1:15, 16; Colossians 2:9; Titus 2:13; Hebrews 1:3, 8; 2 Peter 1:1; 1 John 5:20).
• The Holy Spirit is God (Acts 5:3, 4; 2 Corinthians 3:17; Exodus 34:34; 2 Corinthians 3:16).

# GIFTS *of the* HOLY SPIRIT

The Bible clearly teaches that the Spirit distributes gifts to everyone who believes in Christ. The following is a list of gifts and the chapters where they are found.

| | Rom 12 | 1 Cor 12 | Eph 4 |
|---|---|---|---|
| Apostleship | | X | X |
| Prophecy | X | X | X |
| Evangelism | | | X |
| Pastoring | | | X |
| Teaching | X | X | X |
| Exhortation | X | | |
| Knowledge | | X | |
| Wisdom | | X | |
| Discerning of Spirits | | X | |
| Leadership | X | | |
| Administration | | X | |
| Service/Helps | X | X | |
| Acts of Mercy | X | | |
| Giving | X | | |
| Healing | | X | |
| Faith | | X | |
| Miracles | | X | |
| Speaking & Interpreting Tongues | | X | |
| Miscellaneous: Perhaps Celibacy (Matthew 19:12) Hospitality (Romans 12:13) | | | |

The Holy Spirit gives gifts with particular spiritual functions for the benefit of the entire church. Paul's teaching in 1 Corinthians 12 speaks about the organic unity of Christ's body, the Church. The gifts complement each other and work together for the common good, much as the parts of the body are designed to do. Because this is true, the gifts are given to the church as a whole. It is only within the context of the believing community that the gifts are made to work and only within that community that they can be discovered in the first place.

Our understanding of gifts and gifting depends on how we view the Holy Spirit. He is God's gift to us as individuals and as a body (see Acts 2:38 and 10:45). Individuals who have come into this life, the life of Christ, are automatically part of a larger whole. These gifts operate as parts of a whole. Gifting, reception of the Spirit, and membership in the Body of Christ are all connected in the life of the believer and for the good of the whole church.

### Study Tip

In addition to Paul's list of gifts, the apostle Peter also mentions gifts, dividing them into speaking and serving categories (1 Peter 4:10–11). Compare Paul's list to see how it also divides roughly into half speaking and half serving gifts. The book of Acts is also another great place to see the gifts in action. As you read through the book make a note whenever you encounter the use of one of the gifts listed above.

| Name | References | Meaning |
|------|-----------|---------|
| BREATH OF THE ALMIGHTY | Job 33:4 | The Holy Spirit is the life-giving breath of God. |
| COUNSELOR COMFORTER | John 14:16, 26; 15:26; Romans 8:26 | The Holy Spirit comforts, counsels and gives strength. |
| SPIRIT OF COUNSEL | Isaiah 11:2 | The Holy Spirit counsels and teaches us as we grow in Christ. |
| ETERNAL SPIRIT | Hebrews 9:14 | The Holy Spirit is eternal God. |
| FREE SPIRIT | Psalm 51:12 | The Holy Spirit is God's generous and willing spirit. |
| GOD | Acts 5:3–4 | The Holy Spirit is the Third Person of the Trinity. He is God. |
| GOOD SPIRIT | Nehemiah 9:20; Psalm 143:10 | God's Good Spirit will teach and lead us in all that is good. |
| HOLY SPIRIT | Psalm 51:11; Luke 11:13; Eph. 1:13; 4:30 | God is Spirit and that Spirit is holy. He is the Spirit of holiness. |
| LORD | 2 Cor. 3:16–17 | Like Jesus and the Father, the Holy Spirit is also addressed and worshiped as Lord. |
| POWER OF THE HIGHEST | Luke 1:35 | The Spirit is God's power, the greatest power there is. |
| SPIRIT OF MIGHT | Isaiah 11:2 | The Holy Spirit is the Spirit of Strength. |
| SPIRIT OF ADOPTION | Romans 8:15 | He is the Spirit by which we are made God's children. |
| SPIRIT OF BURNING | Isaiah 4:4 | The Spirit is God's fire of purification. |
| SPIRIT OF JUDGMENT | Isaiah 4:4; 28:6 | The Spirit of God brings conviction and judgment. |
| SPIRIT OF CHRIST (JESUS CHRIST) | Romans 8:9; 1 Peter 1:11 | The Holy Spirit is Jesus' own spirit of love shared with the Father. |
| SPIRIT OF GLORY | 1 Peter 4:14 | The Spirit always gives glory to Christ. |

| Application | Comments |
| --- | --- |
| The Holy Spirit is the source of life from God. He is the one, through Christ, who connects us to God. | The words in both Hebrew and Greek for "wind," "breath," and "spirit" all have similar origins. The idea of flowing life-giving air (see *Spirit of Life*) is what is meant. |
| The Holy Spirit is our strength and comfort. We are to turn to him when we are in trouble and when we are weak, being assured that he intercedes with and for us. | *Paraclete* is the Greek word behind this name. It refers to an advocate, someone called alongside to strengthen and fight on behalf of another (see *Spirit of Counsel*). |
| We need to make use of God's guidance by letting the Holy Spirit lead us and teach us. | Jesus is called the Wonderful Counselor (Isaiah 9:6). Just as the Holy Spirit led Jesus to the wilderness (Luke 4:1), he leads us to truth as our Counselor (John 14:26). |
| The Spirit is no mere created force. He is the timeless Creator who loves us eternally. | The Holy Spirit is co-eternal with God the Father and God the Son. |
| God gives us his willing Spirit to change our hard hearts and give us freedom. | Without God's Spirit who makes us willing to receive him, we would never be free from the prison of sin. |
| The Holy Spirit is not a thing, a force, nor mere power. He is personal, and we are to worship and obey him as God. | We are to understand that God is one in his essence, but three in Person. |
| The Holy Spirit is God's good gift to us for help in the present. | We are not alone in the world. Christ's very own Spirit is with us to work all things for our good. |
| The same Holy Spirit given to us for life is given to make us holy as well. | The term *Holy Ghost* is sometimes used in place of *Holy Spirit*. *Ghost* today has a negative idea attached to it. The use of the qualifier "holy" is to distinguish God's Spirit from evil spirits. |
| The Holy Spirit is God present with us. He is our Lord. | The lordship of the Spirit means we are to obey him and not grieve him. |
| God's power, the Holy Spirit can accomplish things through us that we cannot do ourselves. | The same Greek word for *power* is the word from which we derive *dynamite*. |
| Jesus' Spirit is God's strength given to us. | Jesus told us he would give us the Power of the Spirit (Acts 1:8). |
| God's love toward us as his children comes through the Holy Spirit. As the Spirit persuades us, we become part of God's family. | We may actually refer to God as "Daddy" (*Abba* in Aramaic) or "Father" because we have Jesus' Spirit in us. |
| God's Spirit cleanses and purifies from evil. | The Spirit of God often appears as fire (Matthew 3:11, Acts 2:3). |
| God's Spirit discerns and divides good from evil. | Jesus said the Holy Spirit would convict and judge the world (John 16:8). |
| Jesus has shared the Spirit of love with those who believe him. | The very same Spirit of love that the Father shares with the Son is now given to us (1 John 1:3). |
| Christ's life is what the Spirit focuses us on. | The Holy Spirit is shaping our lives into the glorious pattern of Christ. |

| Name | References | Meaning |
|------|------------|---------|
| SPIRIT OF GOD | Genesis 1:2; 1 Corinthians 2:11; Job 33:4 | The Holy Spirit is the Spirit of the Triune God. |
| SPIRIT OF YAHWEH (SPIRIT OF THE LORD YAHWEH) | Isaiah 11:2; Isaiah 61:1 | The Spirit has the sacred name of God—Yahweh. |
| SPIRIT OF GRACE | Zechariah 12:10; Hebrews 10:29 | God's Spirit is a merciful spirit. |
| SPIRIT OF KNOWLEDGE | Isaiah 11:2 | The Spirit is the Spirit of clarity of mind. |
| SPIRIT OF TRUTH | John 14:17; 15:26 | The Holy Spirit is about truth, not falsehood. |
| SPIRIT OF UNDERSTANDING | Isaiah 11:2 | The Spirit is understanding itself. |
| SPIRIT OF WISDOM | Isaiah 11:2; Ephesians 1:17 | The Holy Spirit is wise. |
| SPIRIT OF LIFE | Romans 8:2 | The Holy Spirit is life-giving (John 6:63). |
| SPIRIT OF THE LIVING GOD | 2 Corinthians 3:3 | The Holy Spirit is the Spirit of the God of life. |
| SPIRIT OF PROPHECY | Revelation 19:10 | It is the Holy Spirit who inspires true prophecy. |
| SPIRIT OF REVELATION | Ephesians 1:17 | God's spirit reveals his truth. |
| SPIRIT OF THE FATHER | Matthew 10:20 | The Holy Spirit is the Spirit of the Father shared with Jesus. |
| SPIRIT OF THE FEAR OF THE LORD | Isaiah 11:2 | The Spirit is the Spirit of reverence toward the Lord. |
| SPIRIT OF THE LORD (GOD) | Acts 5:9 | The Spirit is the presence of the Lord. |
| SPIRIT OF THE SON | Galatians 4:6 | The Spirit is the Spirit of Jesus, the Son, whom he shares with the Father. |
| SPIRIT | Matthew 4:1; John 3:6; 1 Timothy 4:1 | The Holy Spirit is sometimes simply called "Spirit." |

| Application | Comments |
|---|---|
| God is Spirit and truth (John 4:24). | The Holy Spirit is the essence and core of the relationship between the Father and the Son. |
| The Spirit can be called by the sacred name because he is God. | Jesus told his disciples to baptize in the name (singular) of the Father, Son and Holy Spirit (Matthew 28:19). |
| We come to know God's grace only when the Spirit opens our hearts. | Jesus accomplished the work of grace for us on the cross, but it is the Spirit who applies that grace to us by giving us faith. |
| The Spirit does not lead to confusion but to true knowledge (1 Corinthians 14:33). | Jesus is the shoot from Jesse's stem—in other words, the Messiah—that Isaiah prophesied; Jesus had the fullness of the Spirit of knowledge (Isaiah 11:1–2). |
| The Spirit leads us to truth, not error. | Jesus said he is truth. We receive his Spirit of truth. |
| Not merely technical knowledge, the Spirit comprehends and understands our needs. | Jesus said the Spirit would help us understand (John 16:12–15). |
| The Spirit is not merely intellectual, but personal as well: He is wise in the way he leads us. | Wisdom is highly valued by God (see Proverbs). The Spirit is the source of all true wisdom. |
| Just as our biological life requires breath and breathing, we need God's Spirit, his breath to truly live. | Jesus said he is life (John 14:6). His Spirit is the giver of that life. |
| The Spirit of God is living and the giver of life to us. | God is called the Living God because he is life and the source of life through his Spirit to the world. |
| Because the Spirit is the source of prophecy, he helps us understand God's word. | All Scripture is inspired (God-breathed). The Spirit is the breath of inspiration (2 Timothy 3:16). |
| It is the work of the Spirit to reveal God and his truth to us. (See *Spirit of Prophecy* and *Spirit of Truth*.) | Revelation comes from the Father through Jesus by the Spirit who is the voice of God in us. |
| The Spirit of the Father and of Jesus has been sent to us by them. | The Spirit shared between the Father and Son, the Spirit of love, is now given to us. (See *Spirit of Christ* and *Spirit of the Son*.) |
| The Holy Spirit will always lead us to revere God. | God is to be given awe and reverence. It is the Holy Spirit who inspires this attitude in us. |
| We are to worship and obey the Spirit as Lord. | The name indicates the identity of the Spirit as our Lord. |
| The loving Spirit of the Son of God is now given to us. | The Spirit draws us into the love and fellowship that is between the Father and the Son. |
| The Spirit is the integral essence of life, love, and truth. | The Spirit is truly the source of all life; everything that exists does so only because of him. |

# SPIRIT *and* PRAYER

The Spirit of God is the Spirit of prayer. We can only approach God through Christ with the help of the Spirit. Jesus is humanity's only access to God (John 14:6). Since his ascension, Christ has not been physically present on earth; the only way to lay our requests and worship before him, and so before God, is by means of the Holy Spirit.

Jesus promised the gift of the Spirit in the life of his disciples (John 14:16–17) and the Bible tells us that one of the crucial tasks of the Spirit is to inspire and guide our prayers. When our weaknesses prevent us from relating to God correctly, the Spirit intercedes for us—that is, he pleads our case before God (Romans 8:26–27)—so we can rest assured that the Spirit is praying alongside us, making our prayers what they ought to be.

If we understand prayer as communication with God, then we will be able to see it more fully as a dialogue, rather than a monologue on our part. Prayer is a two-way conversation; the other half of our worship before God is God's guidance and clarity of his will to us. Just as we may only reach God in the Spirit through the truth of Christ (John 4:24), so also God's guidance and teaching comes to us only through Christ by means of the Spirit (John 14:26; 15:26; 16:12–14).

# FRUIT *of the* SPIRIT

In Galatians 5:16–25, the Apostle Paul contrasts two different motivations for life: one that allows the sinful nature to lead it, and another that follows the promptings and guidance of the Spirit. The sinful nature produces attitudes and actions that oppose God's will (Galatians 5:19–21). The Spirit naturally leads one to attitudes and actions that are in step with the will of God. Paul calls these attitudes and actions *fruit of the Spirit*. Fruits are the way plants reproduce—they carry the seeds. They are aromatic, colorful and tasty so that they can please and attract carriers of their seed, who spread them and allow the plant to reproduce. The life of a person whom the Spirit leads produces fruit: attitudes and behavior that are pleasing to God and other people. These *fruits of the Spirit* are: **love, joy, peace, patience, kindness, goodness, faithfulness, gentleness and self-control** (Galatians 5: 22–23).

# BAPTISM *of the* HOLY SPIRIT

Different Christian groups define the baptism of the Holy Spirit in different ways.

- For some the idea is intimately connected to water baptism and **initiation** into God's family. Jesus' own baptism seems to set the pattern, where water and the Spirit are both evident (Matthew 3:11–17). Paul speaks of this idea of being initiated into the church this way (1 Corinthians 12:13).

- For others, baptism of the Holy Spirit may be very distinct from water baptism. Here the emphasis is an **infusion** of power for ministry. The book of Acts recounts many instances in which this infusion took place apart from water baptism (Acts 2:4; 4:8).

- Still others regard the Spirit's work as centering on **identification** with Christ. Paul understands baptism and the work of the Spirit as connecting and conforming us to Christ's life by being baptized into or identified with his death (Romans 6:3–4).

In fact, all of these works—initiation, infusion and identification—are involved in the work of the Holy Spirit. His work, his baptism involves all three, though they may not all be in view together at one time. We are initiated into the life and body of Christ by the regenerating act of the Spirit. We are infused with God's power for ministry when the Spirit fills us with himself. We are identified with Christ in his life, death, and resurrection as the Holy Spirit transforms us into Christ's image. All these things may be said to be part of the baptism of the Holy Spirit, for different passages in Scripture direct us to each of these. Yet, there is a sense in which these diverse works are one work of the same Spirit, though we may experience each at different times in our lives. This experiential time difference, coupled with what seems to be different definitions and usage of the term "baptism of the Holy Spirit" in Scripture has led to controversy between Christian groups over this issue.

If we step back to get the larger picture of this singular, timeless work of the Spirit, we may come to see baptism of the Holy Spirit as involving the entire work of the Spirit in, through, and on behalf of humanity.

# BLASPHEMY AGAINST *the* HOLY SPIRIT

Jesus said, *"People will be forgiven for their sins and whatever blasphemies they utter, but whoever blasphemes against the Holy Spirit can never have forgiveness"* (Mark 3:28).

The issue of blasphemy against the Spirit has bothered many Bible readers.

## What is blasphemy against the Holy Spirit?

Blasphemy involves an utterance or action that purposefully defames God. Blasphemies against God are prohibited by the third commandment (Exodus 20:7), yet people regularly misuse God's name and are forgiven. Jesus' name is a target of abuse, yet Christ himself teaches that these offenses may be forgiven (Luke 12:10). What makes blasphemy of the Holy Spirit different?

Jesus seems to be speaking about something bigger than mere words or actions directed against God's Spirit. The context (Mark 3:30) helps us to see that what Jesus' accusers were involved in was insisting that Jesus' Spirit (the Holy Spirit) was at the core demonic, satanic, evil! The point seems to be not that the name calling itself could not be forgiven, but that the ramifications of their words would cause the speakers to reject God's only offer of salvation.

## Why?

Because the Holy Spirit is God's final witness to Christ and his salvation! Whatever one may say of Christ, if the whisper of the Spirit in the ear or the shout of his voice in creation and history is ignored fully and finally, there can be no forgiveness, because there will be no regeneration, no conversion, no repentance.

Blasphemy of the Holy Spirit is thus tied to one of the Spirit's most important works—revelation. In the end, it is the Spirit of Truth, the Spirit of Revelation who must turn the minds and hearts of the human race. If we do not listen to him, we shall never receive Christ, and if we never receive Christ, God will never forgive us.

Author: William Brent Ashby
Editor: Benjamin Galan, MTS, ThM

# The Trinity

What Is the Trinity?

Answers to Misunderstandings

What Early Christians Said about the Trinity

## What Is the Trinity?

# What Christians Believe About the Trinity

In the simplest of terms, Christians believe:

There is only one God, and this one God exists as one essence in three Persons.

The three Persons are    God the Father
God the Son (Jesus Christ)
God the Holy Spirit (also called the Holy Ghost)

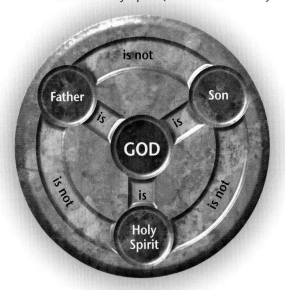

Early Christians used this diagram to explain the Trinity. The Father, Son, and Holy Spirit are all God, but they are not three names for the same Person.

The Persons are distinct:  The Father is not the Son.
The Son is not the Holy Spirit.
The Holy Spirit is not the Father.

## The Trinity and the Bible

God is one absolutely perfect divine Being in three Persons. His *being* is what God *is*, in relation to the universe he created. The three are called Persons because they relate to one another in personal ways.

When Christians talk about believing in one God in three Persons (the Trinity), they do NOT mean:

> 1 God in 3 Gods, or
> 3 Persons in 1 Person, or
> 3 Persons in 3 Gods, or
> 1 Person in 3 Gods

Rather, they mean:

> 1 God in 3 Persons

Therefore,

The Father is God—the first Person
> of the Trinity.

The Son is God—the second Person
> of the Trinity.

The Holy Spirit is God—the third Person
> of the Trinity. (The title "Holy Ghost" is an older English expression for "Holy Spirit." Each is an acceptable translation of the phrase in the Bible.)

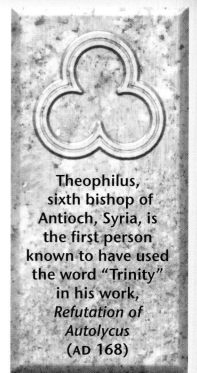

Theophilus, sixth bishop of Antioch, Syria, is the first person known to have used the word "Trinity" in his work, *Refutation of Autolycus* (AD 168)

# Why do Christians Believe in the Trinity?

The Bible clearly teaches that there is only one God, yet all three Persons are called God.

### There is only one God:

- *Hear, O Israel: The LORD our God is one LORD. (Deuteronomy 6:4)*
- *Before me there was no God formed, neither shall there be after me. (Isaiah 43:10)*

### The Father is God:

- *Grace be unto you, and peace, from God our Father and from the Lord Jesus Christ. (1 Corinthians 1:3; 8:6; Ephesians 4:4-6)*

### The Son is God:

- *The Word was God. (John 1:1-5, 14)* Jesus is identified as "the Word."
- *I and the Father are one. (John 10:30-33)*
- Jesus' disciple Thomas addressed Jesus as *"My Lord and my God." (John 20:28)*

  Jesus did not tell Thomas he was mistaken; Instead Jesus accepted these titles. Other people in Scripture, notably Paul and Barnabas (Acts 14), refused to accept worship as gods.

## The Trinity and the Bible

- *But unto the Son he saith, Thy throne, O God, is for ever and ever: a sceptre of righteousness is the sceptre of thy kingdom. (Hebrews 1:6-8)*
- *Wherefore God also hath highly exalted him, and given him a name which is above every name: That at the name of Jesus every knee should bow, of things in heaven, and things in earth, and things under the earth; and that every tongue should confess that Jesus Christ is Lord, to the glory of God the Father. (Philippians 2:9-11)*

  Paul, the writer of Philippians, is saying about Jesus what Isaiah 45:23 says about the LORD, and then Paul concludes that Jesus is LORD, that is, the same LORD God of the Old Testament.

See these passages about Jesus' deity: Isaiah 7:14; Isaiah 9:6; John 1:1; John 1:18; John 8:58, 59; John 10:30; Acts 20:28; Romans 9:5; Romans 10:9-13; Col. 1:15, 16; Colossians 2:9; Titus 2:13; Hebrews 1:3, 8; 2 Peter 1:1; 1 John 5:20.

**The Holy Spirit is God:**

- *But Peter said, Ananias, why hath Satan filled thine heart to lie to the Holy Ghost? ...Thou hast not lied unto men, but unto God. (Acts 5:3-4)*

  This verse equates the Holy Spirit (Holy Ghost) with God.

- *Now the Lord is that Spirit. (2 Corinthians 3:17)*

  "The Lord" here refers to "the LORD" in the Old Testament verse (Ex. 34:34) Paul had just quoted in the previous verse (2 Corinthians 3:16).

## More than 60 Bible passages mention the three Persons together:

- Matthew 3:16, 17 "And Jesus, when he was baptized, went up straightway out of the water: and, lo, the heavens were opened unto him, and he saw the Spirit of God descending like a dove, and lighting upon him: And lo a voice from heaven, saying, This is my beloved Son, in whom I am well pleased."
- Matthew 28:19 "Go ye therefore, and teach all nations, baptizing them in the name of the Father, and of the Son, and of the Holy Ghost."
- 2 Corinthians 13:14 "The grace of the Lord Jesus Christ, and the love of God, and the communion of the Holy Ghost, be with you all."
- Ephesians 4:4-6 "There is one body, and one Spirit, even as ye are called in one hope of your calling; one Lord, one faith, one baptism, one God and Father of all, who is above all, and through all, and in you all."
- Titus 3:4-6 "But after that the kindness and love of God our Saviour toward man appeared, not by works of righteousness which we have done, but according to his mercy he saved us, by the washing of regeneration, and renewing of the Holy Ghost; which he shed on us abundantly through Jesus Christ our Saviour . . ."

See also John 3:34, 35; John 14:26; John 15:26; John 16:13-15; Romans 14:17, 18; Romans 15:13-17; Romans 15:30; 1 Corinthians 6:11, 17-19; 1 Corinthians 12:4-6; 2 Corinthians 1:21, 22; 2 Cor. 3:4-6; Galatians 2:21-3:2; Galatians 4:6; Ephesians 2:18; Ephesians 3:11-17; Ephesians 5:18-20; Colossians 1:6-8; 1 Thessalonians 1:1-5; 1 Thessalonians 4:2, 8; 1 Thessalonians 5:18, 19; 2 Thessalonians 3:5; Hebrews 9:14; 1 Peter 1:2; 1 John 3:23, 24; 1 John 4:13, 14; and Jude 20, 21.

## Misunderstandings About the Trinity

### Misunderstanding #1: "The word 'Trinity' does not appear in the Bible; it is a belief made up by Christians in the 4th century."

Truth: It is true that the word "Trinity" does not appear in the Bible, but the Trinity is nevertheless a Bible-based belief. The word "incarnation" does not appear in the Bible either, but we use it as a one-word summary of our belief that Jesus was God in the flesh.

The word "Trinity" was used to explain the eternal relationship between the Father, the Son, and the Holy Spirit. Many Bible passages express the Trinity (page 38). False beliefs flourished during the early days of Christianity, and still do. Early Christians constantly defended their beliefs. The following early church leaders and/or writings all defended the doctrine of the Trinity long before AD 300:

Approximate Dates:

| | |
|---|---|
| AD 96 | **Clement**, the third bishop of Rome |
| AD 90-100 | **The Teachings of the Twelve Apostles**, the "Didache" |
| AD 90? | **Ignatius**, bishop of Antioch |
| AD 155 | **Justin Martyr**, great Christian writer |
| AD 168 | **Theophilus**, the sixth bishop of Antioch |
| AD 177 | **Athenagoras**, theologian |
| AD 180 | **Irenaeus**, bishop of Lyons |
| AD 197 | **Tertullian**, early church leader |
| AD 264 | **Gregory Thaumaturgus**, early church leader |

### Misunderstanding #2: "Christians believe there are three Gods."

Truth: Christians believe in only one God.

Some people might believe that Christians are polytheists (people who believe in many gods) because Christians refer to the Father as God, the Son as God, and the Holy Spirit as God. But Christians believe in only one God. The Bible says there is only one God. But it also calls three distinct Persons "God." Over the centuries people have tried to come up with simple explanations for the Trinity. There are limits to every illustration, but some are helpful. For example, it has been said that

| | |
|---|---|
| God is not | $1 + 1 + 1 = 3$ |
| God is | $1 \times 1 \times 1 = 1$ |

The Trinity is a profound doctrine that must be accepted by faith. Accepting a doctrine by faith does not exclude reason, but it also means that we cannot always apply the same logic that we use in mathematics. Without the Trinity, the Christian doctrine of salvation cannot stand. Some religious groups that claim to believe in the God of the Bible, but reject the Trinity, have an understanding of salvation that is based on good works.

St. Patrick is believed to have used the shamrock as a way of illustrating the Trinity. He asked, "Is this one leaf or three? If one leaf, why are there three lobes of equal size? If three leaves, why is there just one stem? If you cannot explain so simple a mystery as the shamrock, how can you hope to understand one so profound as the Holy Trinity?" Even though this is an overly simple way to explain the Trinity, some teachers find it helpful.

*St. Patrick (AD 432) used the shamrock to illustrate the Trinity.*

## Misunderstandings About the Trinity

### Misunderstanding #3: "Jesus is not God."

Truth: Jesus is God, the Second Person of the Trinity.

### 1. Jesus' own claims

- **He forgave sin.** We may forgive sins committed against us, but we cannot forgive sins committed against others. Jesus has the authority to forgive any sin. (Mark 2:5-12; Luke 5:21)
- **He accepted worship as God and claimed to deserve the same honor as the Father.** (Matthew 14:33; 28:17, 18; John 5:22, 23; 9:38; 17:5)
- **He claimed to be the divine Son of God,** a title the Jews rightly understood to be a claim to equality with God. (John 5:17, 18; 10:30-33; 19:7)

**2.**

| Traits Unique to God | Traits of Jesus |
|---|---|
| Creation is "the work of his hands"—alone (Genesis 1:1; Psalm 102:25; Isaiah 44:24) | Creation is "the work of his hands"—all things created in and through him (John 1:3; Colossians 1:16; Hebrews 1:2, 10) |
| "The first and the last" (Isaiah 44:6) | "The first and the last" (Revelation 1:17; 22:13) |
| "Lord of lords" (Deuteronomy 10:17; Psalm 136:3) | "Lord of lords" (1 Timothy 6:15; Revelation 17:14; 19:16) |
| Unchanging and eternal (Psalm 90:2; 102:26, 27; Malachi 3:6) | Unchanging and eternal (John 8:58; Colossians 1:17; Hebrews 1:11-12; 13:8) |
| Judge of all people (Genesis 18:25; Psalms 94:2; 96:13; 98:9) | Judge of all people (John 5:22; Acts 17:31; 2 Cor. 5:10; 2 Timothy 4:1) |
| Only Savior; no other God can save (Isaiah 43:11; 45:21, 22; Hosea 13:4) | Savior of the world; no salvation apart from him (John 4:42; Acts 4:12; Titus 2:13; 1 John 4:14) |
| Redeems from their sins a people for his own possession (Exodus 19:5; Psalm 130:7, 8; Ezekiel 37:23) | Redeems from their sins a people for his own possession (Titus 2:14) |
| Hears and answers prayers of those who call on him (Psalm 86:5-8; Isaiah 55:6, 7; Jer. 33:3; Joel 2:32) | Hears and answers prayers of those who call on him (John 14:14; Romans 10:12, 13; 1 Corinthians 1:2; 2 Corinthians 12:8, 9) |
| Only God has divine glory (Isaiah 42:8; 48:11) | Jesus has divine glory (John 17:5) |
| Worshiped by angels (Psalm 97:7) | Worshiped by angels (Hebrews 1:6) |

## Misunderstandings About the Trinity

### Misunderstanding #4: "Jesus is a *lesser* God than the Father."

Truth: Jesus is co-equal with God the Father. People who deny this truth may use the following arguments and verses. (These heresies date back to Arius, AD 319.)

### Verses wrongly used to teach that Christ was created:

1. Colossians 1:15: If Christ is "the firstborn of all creation," was he created?

   Answer: "Firstborn" cannot mean that Christ was created, because Paul says that all of creation was made in and for Christ, and that he exists before all creation and holds it together (Colossians 1:16, 17). The "firstborn" traditionally was the main heir. In context Paul is saying that Christ, as God's Son, is the main heir of all creation (verses 12-14).

2. John 3:16: Does "only begotten Son" mean Jesus had a beginning?

   Answer: "Only-begotten" does not mean that Jesus had a beginning; it means that Jesus is God's "unique" Son. In Hebrews 11:17, Isaac is called Abraham's "unique" son, even though Abraham had other children (Genesis 22:2; 25:1-6). Jesus is God's unique Son because only Jesus is fully God and eternally the Father's Son (John 1:1-3, 14-18).

3. Proverbs 8:22: Does this mean that Christ ("Wisdom") was "created"?

   Answer: This is not a literal description of Christ; it is a personification of wisdom. For example, Christ did not dwell in heaven with someone named Prudence (verse 12); he did not build a house with seven pillars (9:1). This verse says in a poetic way that God used wisdom in creating the world (see Proverbs 3:19, 20).

### Verses wrongly used to teach that Jesus is inferior to the Father:

1. John 14:28: If "the Father is greater than" Jesus, how can Jesus be God?

   Answer: In his human life on earth Jesus voluntarily shared our natural limitations in order to save us. After he rose from the dead, Jesus returned to the glory he had with the Father (John 17:5; Philippians 2:9-11). In that restored glory, Jesus was able to send the Holy Spirit and empower his disciples to do even greater works than Jesus did while he was here in the flesh (John 14:12, 26-28).

2. 1 Corinthians 15:28: If Jesus is God, why will he be subject to the Father?

   Answer: Jesus humbly and voluntarily submits himself to the Father's will for a time (Philippians 2:5-11). But, as the pre-existent and eternal Son, he is co-equal with God the Father.

3. Mark 13:32: If Jesus is God, how could he not know when he would return?

   Answer: Jesus voluntarily lowered himself to experience the limitations of human life. Paradoxically, while Jesus continued to be God, he chose to limit his access to knowledge (John 16:30). Paradoxes like this (not contradictions) are exactly what we would expect if, as the Bible says, God chose to live as a real human being (John 1:1, 14).

## Misunderstandings About the Trinity

**Misunderstanding #5:** "The Father, the Son, and the Spirit are just different titles for Jesus, or three different ways that God has revealed himself."

Truth: The Bible clearly shows that the Father, Son, and Holy Spirit are distinct persons.

Some people think that the doctrine of the Trinity contradicts the truth that there is only one God. They argue that Jesus alone is the one true God, and therefore that Jesus is "the name of the Father and the Son and the Holy Spirit" (Matthew 28:19), and not just the name of the Son. While it is certainly true that there is only one God, we must allow the Bible to define what this means. And the Bible makes it quite clear that the Father, Son, and Holy Spirit are distinct persons:

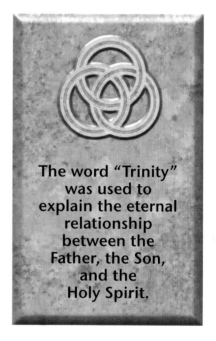

**The word "Trinity" was used to explain the eternal relationship between the Father, the Son, and the Holy Spirit.**

• The Father sends the Son (1 John 4:14; Galatians 4:4)
• The Father sends the Spirit (John 14:26; Galatians 4:6)
• The Son speaks, not on his own, but on behalf of the Father (John 8:28; 12:49)
• The Spirit speaks, not on his own, but on behalf of Jesus (John 16:13-15)
• The Father loves the Son, and the Son loves the Father (John 3:35; 5:20; 14:31)
• The Father and the Son count as two witnesses (John 5:31-37; 8:16-18)
• The Father and the Son glorify one another (John 17:1,4, 5), and the Spirit glorifies Jesus the Son (John 16:14)
• The Son is an Advocate for us with the Father (1 John 2:1; Greek, *parakletos*); Jesus the Son sent the Holy Spirit, who is another Advocate (John 14:16, 26)
• Jesus Christ is not the Father, but the Son of the Father (2 John 3)

In Matthew 28:19, Jesus is not identifying himself as the Father, Son, and Holy Spirit. He is saying that Christian baptism identifies a person as one who believes in the Father, in the Son whom the Father sent to die for our sins, and in the Holy Spirit whom the Father and the Son sent to dwell in our hearts.

## Misunderstandings About the Trinity

### Misunderstanding #6: "Jesus wasn't really fully God and fully man."

Throughout history many people have balked at the idea that Jesus is both fully God and fully man. They have tried to resolve this paradox by saying that Jesus was a mere man through whom God spoke, or that he was God and merely appeared to be human, or some other "simpler" belief. Admittedly the idea that in Jesus, God became a man, is difficult for us to comprehend. But the Incarnation— the truth that God became flesh—is the ultimate proof that nothing is too hard for God (Genesis 18:14; Luke 1:37). And this truth is clearly taught in the Bible.

### The Bible clearly shows that Jesus was fully human:

As a child, he grew physically, intellectually, socially, and spiritually (Luke 2:40, 52).

He grew tired; he slept; he sweat; he was hungry and thirsty; he bled and died; his body was buried (Matthew 4:2; 8:24; Luke 22:44; John 4:6, 7; 19:28-42).

After he rose from the dead, he ate and drank with people and let them see his scars and touch his body (Luke 24:39-43; John 20:27-29; Acts 10:41).

### The Bible also clearly shows that Jesus was fully God:

Jesus did on earth what only God can do: he commanded the forces of nature (Matthew 8:23-27; 14:22, 33); forgave sins (Mark 2:1-12); claimed to be superior to the Sabbath law (John 5:17, 18); and gave life to whomever he pleased (John 5:19-23).

Paul said that God purchased the church with his own blood (Acts 20:28).

Paul also said that the rulers of this world unwittingly crucified the Lord of glory (1 Corinthians 2:8).

All the fullness of God's nature and being resides in Jesus' risen body (Colossians 2:9).

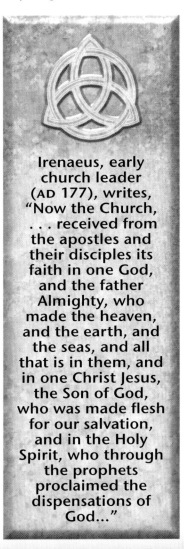

Irenaeus, early church leader (AD 177), writes, "Now the Church, . . . received from the apostles and their disciples its faith in one God, and the father Almighty, who made the heaven, and the earth, and the seas, and all that is in them, and in one Christ Jesus, the Son of God, who was made flesh for our salvation, and in the Holy Spirit, who through the prophets proclaimed the dispensations of God..."

## How Early Christians Dealt with These Misunderstandings

Early Christian theologians of the first two centuries wrote many works defending Christianity from several threats:

- Persecution from the Roman Empire. Until the early AD 300s, Christianity was illegal and often Christians were viciously persecuted.
- Heresies attacking basic Christian beliefs, especially the deity of Jesus Christ and the nature of God.

The **Apostles' Creed** was one of the earliest statements of faith Christian leaders crafted to clarify basic Christian beliefs. It emphasizes the true humanity—including the physical body—of Jesus, which was the belief the heretics of the time denied.

*I believe in God, the Father almighty, Creator of heaven and earth, and in Jesus Christ, his only Son, our Lord, who was conceived by the Holy Spirit, born of the Virgin Mary, suffered under Pontius Pilate, was crucified, died and was buried; he descended into hell;*

*on the third day he rose again from the dead; he ascended into heaven, and is seated at the right hand of God the Father almighty;*

*from there he will come to judge the living and the dead. I believe in the Holy Spirit, the holy catholic Church, the communion of saints, the forgiveness of sins, the resurrection of the body, and life everlasting. Amen.*

The **Nicene Creed** was written by church leaders in AD 325, and was later expanded somewhat. It was written to defend the church's belief in Christ's full deity and to reject formally the teachings of Arius, a man who claimed that Jesus was a created, inferior deity.

*We believe in one God, the Father, the Almighty, maker of heaven and earth, of all that is, seen and unseen.*

*We believe in one Lord, Jesus Christ, the only Son of God, eternally begotten of the Father, Light from Light, true God from true God, begotten, not made, of one Being with the Father; through him all things were made. For us and for our salvation he came down from heaven; by the power of the Holy Spirit he became incarnate from the virgin Mary and was made man. For our sake he was crucified under Pontius Pilate; he suffered death and was buried; on the third day he rose again in accordance with the Scriptures; he ascended into heaven. He is seated at the right hand of the Father, he will come again in glory to judge the living and the dead, and his kingdom will have no end.*

*We believe in the Holy Spirit, the Lord, the giver of life, who proceeds from the Father and the Son; with the Father and the Son he is worshiped and glorified; he has spoken through the prophets.*

*We believe in one holy catholic and apostolic Church. We acknowledge one baptism for the forgiveness of sins. We look for the resurrection of the dead, and the life of the world to come.*

Note: The Greek word from which the word *catholic* is derived means "universal." The "catholic Church" means the ancient church that agreed with the whole of the apostles' teaching, as opposed to false teachers that followed a "secret revelation" or emphasized only one part of the first century apostles' teachings.

# The Church and the Creeds

The **Athanasian Creed,** written about AD 400 and named after Athanasius, a great defender of the Trinity, says the three Persons are not three Gods, but only one.

*This is what the catholic faith teaches: we worship one God in the Trinity and the Trinity in unity. We distinguish among the persons, but we do not divide the substance.*

*For the Father is a distinct person; the Son is a distinct person; and the Holy Spirit is a distinct person. Still the Father and the Son and the Holy Spirit have one divinity, equal glory, and coeternal majesty. What the Father is, the Son is, and the Holy Spirit is.*

*The Father is uncreated, the Son is uncreated, and the Holy Spirit is uncreated. The Father is boundless, the Son is boundless, and the Holy Spirit is boundless. The Father is eternal, the Son is eternal, and the Holy Spirit is eternal.*

*Nevertheless, there are not three eternal beings, but one eternal being. Thus there are not three uncreated beings, nor three boundless beings, but one uncreated being and one boundless being. Likewise, the Father is omnipotent, the Son is omnipotent, and the Holy Spirit is omnipotent. Yet there are not three omnipotent beings, but one omnipotent being.*

*Thus the Father is God, the Son is God, and the Holy Spirit is God. But there are not three gods, but one God. The Father is Lord, the Son is Lord, and the Holy Spirit is Lord. There as not three lords, but one Lord.*

*For according to Christian truth, we must profess that each of the persons individually is God; and according to Christian religion we are forbidden to say there are three Gods or three Lords.*

*The Father is made of none, neither created nor begotten. The Son is of the Father alone; not made nor created, but begotten. The Holy Spirit is of the Father and of the Son; neither made, nor created, nor begotten, but proceeding.*

*So there is one Father, not three Fathers; one Son, not three Sons; one Holy Spirit, not three Holy Spirits. And in this Trinity none is afore, nor after another; none is greater, or less than another.*

*But the whole three persons are co-eternal, and co-equal. So that in all things, as aforesaid, the Unity in Trinity and the Trinity in Unity is to be worshipped.*

The **Chalcedonian Creed,** written in AD 451 by church leaders to defend the faith against false teachings, says that Jesus is fully God and fully man.

*Therefore, following the holy fathers, we all with one accord teach men to acknowledge one and the same Son, our Lord Jesus Christ, at once complete in Godhead and complete in manhood, truly God and truly man, consisting also of a reasonable soul and body; of one substance (homoousios) with the Father as regards his Godhead, and at the same time of one substance with us as regards his manhood; like us in all respects, apart from sin; as regards his Godhead, begotten of the Father before the ages, but yet as regards his manhood begotten, for us men and for our salvation, of Mary the Virgin, the God-bearer (theotokos); one and the same Christ, Son, Lord, Only-begotten, recognized in two natures, without confusion, without change, without division, without separation; the distinction of natures being in no way annulled by the union, but rather the characteristics of each nature being preserved and coming together to form one person and subsistence, not as parted or separated into two persons, but one and the same Son and Only-begotten God the Word, Lord Jesus Christ; even as the prophets from earliest times spoke of him, and our Lord Jesus Christ himself taught us, and the creed of the Fathers has handed down to us.*

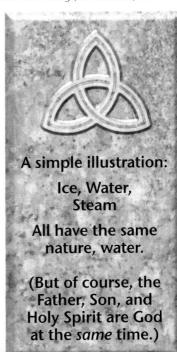

A simple illustration:

Ice, Water, Steam

All have the same nature, water.

(But of course, the Father, Son, and Holy Spirit are God at the *same* time.)

# Important Bible Verses and References

| Divine Attributes | Father | Son | Holy Spirit |
|---|---|---|---|
| Eternal | Romans 16:26, 27 | Revelation 1:17 | Hebrews 9:14 |
| Creator of all things | Psalm 100:3 | Colossians 1:16 | Psalm 104:30 |
| Omnipresent (capable of being all places at once) | Jeremiah 23:24 | Ephesians 1:23 | Psalm 139:7 |
| Omniscient (knows all things) | 1 John 3:20 | John 21:17 | 1 Corinthians 2:10 |
| Wills and acts supernaturally | Ephesians 1:5 | Matthew 8:3 | 1 Corinthians 12:11 |
| Gives life | Genesis 1:11-31 see also John 5:21 | John 1:4 see also John 5:21 | Romans 8:10, 11 see also John 3:8 |
| Strengthens believers | Psalm 138:3 | Philippians 4:13 | Ephesians 3:16 |

## For Further Reading

Beisner, E. Calvin. *God in Three Persons*. Wheaton: Tyndale House, 1984. Popular overview of the historical development of the doctrine.

Bickersteth, Edward H. *The Trinity*. Grand Rapids: Kregel, 1957. Classic exposition of the doctrine from a multitude of biblical texts.

Bowman, Robert M., Jr. *Why You Should Believe in the Trinity*. Grand Rapids: Baker, 1989. Answers to various criticisms of the doctrine.

Boyd, Gregory A. *Oneness Pentecostals and the Trinity*. Grand Rapids: Baker, 1992. Biblical critique of the belief held by Oneness Pentecostals that Jesus is the Father, Son, and Holy Spirit.

Bray, Gerald. *Creeds, Councils and Christ*. Downers Grove, IL: InterVarsity Press, 1984. More advanced analysis of the origins and biblical basis of the creeds.

Reymond, Robert L. *Jesus, Divine Messiah: The New Testament Witness*. Phillipsburg, NJ: Presbyterian & Reformed, 1990. Advanced biblical study, defending Christ's deity primarily against modern critical theories.

Rhodes, Ron. *Christ Before the Manger*. Grand Rapids: Baker, 1992. What the Bible says about Jesus before he became a man. Also see Rhodes's book *The Complete Book of Bible Answers*.

## Helpful Websites

www.watchman.org/subindex.htm

Watchman Fellowship, P.O. Box 13340, Arlington, TX 76094, Ph. (800) 769-2824

Specializes in teaching biblical interpretation and in tracking numerous religious groups that deny the Trinity and other essential Christian doctrines (Scroll down to *Trinity* in this alphabetical list of topics.)

www.blueletterbible.org/Comm/robert_bowman/trinity.html

Blue Letter Bible, 22431 Antonio Pkwy, Suite B160-618, Rancho Santa Margarita, CA 92688-3932

On-line interactive reference library continuously updated from the teachings and commentaries of selected pastors and teachers.

www.apologeticsindex.org/t10.html

Apologetics Index (contact: Anton Hein) Online literature explaining a variety of Christian doctrines.

www.irr.org/mit/trinity1.html

Institute for Religious Research (contact: Luke P. Wilson), 1340 Monroe Ave. NW, Grand Rapids, MI 49505 Ph. (616) 451-4562

Scripture taken from the HOLY BIBLE: KING JAMES VERSION
Contributors: Robert M. Bowman, Jr; Dennis L. Okholm, PhD; Gary M. Burge, PhD; Paul Carden; Robert Cubillos; Ron Rhodes, PhD

# The Ten Commandments

What Are the Ten Commandments?

How Did They Come to Us?

Are They Relevant for Today?

# THE COMMANDMENTS: THEN AND NOW

The set of rules, the Ten Commandments, are the code of law given by God directly to Moses on Mount Sinai. After the Exodus, when God delivered the Israelites from slavery in Egypt, His chosen people almost immediately lost sight of God's power and goodness to them. They resented their hardships and began to complain. They became quarrelsome and difficult to govern. Moses sought God's help on Mount Sinai (Exodus 15–18).

## The Old Testament

God Himself engraved His will for the people on two tablets of stone. The first group of commandments laid out the rules to protect the harmony between God and people; the second group was designed to maintain respect between people. It was vital to the stability of the forming tribal nation that everyone act in a trustworthy manner. Selfishness risked the community's survival. When a person broke a commandment, he had to pay a penalty, repay the person he had injured, and make a sacrifice to restore peace with God.

The Law must be viewed as a great, gracious gift from the God of Israel to His people. Unlike all the other ancient near eastern gods, the Lord God revealed His will and made it very clear how to please Him and how to properly conduct one's life in order to get along in society. Despite the gift of these divine commands for governing relationships, the people set up idols and worshipped them, they lied and stole from one another; many of their leaders were corrupt, and they refused to honor God. Over the next 1400 years, the law was often forgotten and the worship of the true God was abandoned. God called to the people. Sometimes they would return to God and be restored. Other times they would ignore Him and suffer devastating hardships.

The Lord said that someday He would send a Savior and would have a new covenant with His people. The law would be written on their hearts, not just on stone tablets. They would do the right thing because they loved God (Jeremiah 31:31-33).

## The New Testament (New Covenant)

God sent a Savior, Jesus Christ, to live a perfect life and take the penalty for sin through His death on the cross. Through His sacrifice, He made forgiveness and friendship with God possible, and made us perfect in God's eyes through faith (Romans 3:20; Galatians 2:16, 3:9 –14). Jesus came to fulfill the law, and taught that the spirit of the law was as important as the letter of the law (Matthew 23:23).

*"By this we know that we love the children of God, when we love God and observe His commandments. For this is the love of God, that we keep His commandments; and His commandments are not burdensome."* —1 John 5:2-3 NASB

THE PRINCIPLE ▷

WHAT DOES IT MEAN? ▷

IN THE BIBLE ▷

JESUS' TEACHINGS ▷

EXPLANATIONS ▷

# 1 No Other God
## THOU SHALT HAVE NO OTHER GODS BEFORE ME.

## GOD IS THE CREATOR AND LORD OF THE UNIVERSE. HE DESERVES OUR FIRST LOYALTY.

Put God first and give Him our devotion. God should always be our highest priority, over everyone and everything. A god is anything a person allows to rule his or her life. Other gods could include: deities of other religions, superstitions, horoscopes, money, possessions, career, personal comfort, family, friends, addictions, fame, power, security, romance, sex, church, extreme patriotism—anything that comes before God.

- Abraham proved that God was his first priority by being willing to give up his own son (Genesis 22:1-14).
- The people of Israel were worshiping other gods, so the prophet Elijah challenged the prophets of those gods to a contest. Elijah prayed that God would answer him so all would know that the LORD is God. The LORD answered and proved His superiority (1 Kings 18:20-40).
- God commanded the prophet Hosea to marry a prostitute who was unfaithful to him, so that Hosea might understand how God feels when His people turn to other gods (Hosea 1–3).
- Daniel and his three friends, Shadrach, Meshach, and Abednego, risked their lives because they remained devoted to the LORD as their only God (Daniel 1; 3; 6).

When asked, "Which is the greatest commandment in the Law?" Jesus replied: "Love the Lord your God with all your heart and with all your soul and with all your mind. This is the first and greatest commandment" (Matthew 22:26-38).

In the Sermon on the Mount Jesus said, "No one can serve two masters. Either he will hate the one and love the other, or he will be devoted to the one and despise the other. You cannot serve both God and Money" (Matthew 6:24).

Jesus said, "Worship the Lord your God, and serve him only" (Luke 4:8).

Jesus said that all the commandments and rules in the Bible hang on two basic principles:
1. **Loving God with all of your heart, mind, soul, and strength (First four commandments).**
2. **Loving your neighbor as yourself (Next six commandments).**

In the Old Testament, people were offering sacrifices to God because the law commanded them to do so. God wanted sacrifices and burnt offerings as an outward sign of a right heart attitude. God wants to be acknowledged, and He wants people to show mercy to others (Hosea 6:6). God wants us to obey the laws and rules He gives us because we treasure Him and we want to serve Him.

# 2 No Idols

## THOU SHALT NOT MAKE UNTO THEE ANY GRAVEN IMAGE.

**PRINCIPLE**

## GOD IS SPIRIT AND IS BIGGER AND MORE POWERFUL THAN ANY REPRESENTATION.

**MEANING**

Put faith in God only. Idol worship is worshiping or serving anything in the place of God. Idolatry can also include the worship of the true God *through* an idol. God does not forbid or condemn all representations of people and animals. God commanded that ornamental artwork be made in order to make things beautiful. When we worship something we can see, touch, or control, we miss the power and grandeur of God.

**BIBLE EXAMPLES**

- The prophet Habakkuk wrote that idolatry is when man trusts his own creation more than he trusts God (Habakkuk 2:18, 19).
- While Moses was receiving the Ten Commandments, the Israelites created a golden calf, bowed down, and sacrificed offerings to it. God became very angry with them (Ex. 32:1-24).
- Gideon made an idol, which became a snare for his family, because Israel worshiped the idol instead of God (Judges 8:26, 27).
- The prophet Isaiah spoke of idol worship, saying a man will burn a tree for warmth or cooking while using the same tree to fashion an idol for worship (Isaiah 44:9-20).
- The Apostle Paul associated idolatry with impurity, lust, evil desires and greed (Colossians 3:5).

**JESUS' TEACHINGS**

Jesus said, "Do not store up for yourselves treasures on earth, where moth and rust destroy, and where thieves break in and steal" (Matthew 6:19).

Jesus said, "For everyone who exalts himself will be humbled, and he who humbles himself will be exalted" (Matthew 18:14).

When Jesus met the Samaritan woman at the well, she asked whether to worship God in Jerusalem or Samaria. He said, "Yet a time is coming and has now come when the true worshippers will worship the Father in spirit and truth, for they are the kind of worshippers the Father seeks. God is spirit, and his worshippers must worship in spirit and in truth" (John 4:23, 24).

**EXPLANATIONS**

God instructed Moses to build a Tabernacle that contained furniture overlaid with bronze or gold, a solid gold lampstand, and the ark of the covenant overlaid with gold (Exodus 25:1–27:21). Solomon had Hiram the Bronzeworker mold a bronze sea (basin) and had it placed upon twelve bronze oxen statues (1 Kings 7:23-26). God gives many people the gift of craftsmanship and the abilities to make beautiful images. To sculpt, paint, or design something can bring glory to God. Yet, God is spirit and cannot be represented by any image crafted by human hands. To do so would be an insult to the very nature of God. God also desires that we worship Him in spirit, and not through something we ourselves created (John 4:23, 24).

# 3 DO NOT MISUSE GOD'S NAME
## THOU SHALT NOT TAKE THE NAME OF THE LORD THY GOD IN VAIN.

## GOD'S NAME IS HOLY, POWERFUL, AND GLORIOUS.

God's name is holy and should be treated with respect. There is power in the LORD's name and it shouldn't be used lightly. Because God is Spirit, we know Him through what He says about Himself; to take His name in vain violates God's nature. As God's creation, everything a person says and does should be done in order to praise and glorify God (1 Corinthians 10:31).

- When a man named Shelomith blasphemed the name of God with a curse, the Lord commanded that he be taken outside the camp and stoned to death (Leviticus 24:10-16).
- Jesus was accused of blasphemy because He claimed to be God (John 10:33).
- The high priest claimed that Jesus broke the third commandment by claiming to be God, and condemned Jesus to death for this blasphemy (Matthew 25:63-68; 27:39-43; John 10:33).
- James warned believers to watch what they say because the tongue is capable of evil and poison and can easily corrupt a person (James 3:5-9).

Jesus said, "…every sin and blasphemy will be forgiven men, but the blasphemy against the Spirit will not be forgiven … But I tell you that men will have to give account on the day of judgment for every careless word they have spoken. For by your words you will be acquitted, and by your words you will be condemned" (Matthew 12:31, 36, 37).

Jesus said to begin praying with: "Our Father in heaven, hallowed be your name" (Matthew 6:9). In the Sermon on the Mount Jesus said, "Do not swear at all: either by heaven, for it is God's throne; or by the earth, for it is his footstool … Simply let your 'Yes' be 'Yes,' and your 'No,' 'No'; anything beyond this comes from the evil one" (Matthew 5:33-35, 37).

Jews and Jewish scribes would go to great measures in order to avoid saying or writing the LORD's name for fear of blasphemy. The Bible says we are to pray, heal, and baptize in Jesus' name (Matthew 28:19; Mark 16:17; John 14:13; 16:23; Acts 3:6).

The Bible says that what we say is very important and it is a glimpse into who we are (James 3:9-12). God loves us and wants us to love and worship Him in whatever we are doing and at all times. God wants us to use His name; it is holy and powerful. If we can show respect for the names of our fathers, mothers, teachers, and doctors, then how much more should we respect the name of our sovereign God.

# 4 REST ON THE SABBATH
## REMEMBER THE SABBATH DAY, TO KEEP IT HOLY.

**PRINCIPLE**

## GOD VALUES REST, SPIRITUAL REFRESHMENT, AND TIME FOR HIS PEOPLE TO WORSHIP HIM.

**MEANING**

As a gift, God gives all people a day to rest after six days of labor. God knew how to preserve His creation, and rest was a necessary component to that preservation. Without rest, valuable topsoil is used up and the land becomes useless. In the same way, without rest, human beings become unproductive. Without spiritual refreshment, we can have rested bodies inhabited by unrested minds. The very center of rest is the worship of God. It is where we find our fulfillment because worship is what we were made for. The Sabbath day is an opportunity to renew our relationship with God and refocus on Him by honoring Him in our worship.

**BIBLE EXAMPLES**

- The Sabbath was ordained in creation and ordered by God even before the commandments were given on Mount Sinai (Genesis 2:2, 3; Exodus 16:23-29).
- Death was the prescribed punishment for working on the Sabbath (Exodus 35:2-4).
- The prophet Isaiah wrote that God detested meaningless sacrifices and empty obedience to religious festivals, to new moon celebrations, and to the Sabbath day (Isaiah 1:11-13).
- God instituted seven holidays as sacred assemblies and special Sabbath days. These included: Passover, Unleavened Bread, Firstfruits, Weeks, Trumpets, Day of Atonement, and Tabernacles (Leviticus 21:1, 2).
- Every 50th year was to be a sabbath year, the year of Jubilee, in which the land would not be tilled, slaves were freed, and alienated property restored (Leviticus 25:8-33).

**JESUS' TEACHINGS**

One day Jesus started healing people on the Sabbath and many people came to Him to be healed. The synagogue ruler told the people to come back and be healed on any day but the Sabbath. The ruler thought healing on the Sabbath was a violation of the fourth commandment. Jesus rebuked him and told the people that it is acceptable to have mercy on someone on the Sabbath, even if it may appear to violate the law (Luke 13:15, 16).

Jesus said, "The Sabbath was made for man, not man for the Sabbath. So the Son of Man is Lord even of the Sabbath" (Mark 2:27, 28). In this way, Jesus declared that a person may do good on the Sabbath.

**EXPLANATIONS**

In the Old Testament, the Sabbath day was observed on Saturday, the seventh day of the week, because God rested on the seventh day after creating the universe. Jesus rose from the dead on Sunday morning, the first day of the week. Through Christ's death and resurrection, He instituted a new creation (Galatians 6:14-16). Since Christ's resurrection, most believers have been recognizing Sunday as "the Lord's day" on which tithes are given and the Lord's Supper is celebrated (Acts 20:7; 1 Corinthians 16; Revelation 1:10).

Some suggest that followers of Jesus should still observe the Sabbath on Saturday rather than on Sunday. Others suggest that the Sabbath can happen on any day of the week. The Sabbath is to be a holy day, to rest, refocus, and praise God for creating us anew in Christ.

# 5 HONOR YOUR PARENTS

HONOUR THY FATHER AND THY MOTHER: THAT THY DAYS MAY BE
LONG UPON THE LAND WHICH THE LORD THY GOD GIVETH THEE.

## GOD WANTS ALL PEOPLE TO RESPECT AND HONOR THOSE HE'S PLACED IN AUTHORITY.

Treat parents with respect, no matter what the situation may be. Most parents made great
sacrifices to bring up their children. No one is a perfect parent, and in some cases, fathers and
mothers are dishonorable and have caused pain and grief. Even in these cases, when parents
may not deserve it, God expects us to honor them for His sake. God promises long life to
those who honor their parents. Scripture also makes it clear that sometimes we must follow
God instead of obeying parents.

- King Solomon wrote that wisdom comes from obeying one's parents (Proverbs 23:22-26).
- Jesus was obedient to His earthly parents as He grew up in Nazareth (Luke 2:51).
- The Apostle Paul commanded children to obey their parents in everything, and he
  reminded them that the fifth commandment contained a promise. If children honor their
  parents they will enjoy long life (Ephesians 6:1-3; Colossians 3:20).
- After the flood, Noah became intoxicated. Seeing Noah in this condition, his son Ham
  made fun of him to his brothers, Shem and Japheth. Even though Noah was
  irresponsible, Ham received a curse for dishonoring his father. Shem and Japheth were
  blessed because they honored their father (Genesis 9:20-27).

Jesus rebuked the Jewish authorities of His day for not taking care of their aging parents.
He said that they made up excuses in order to avoid having to honor their parents
(Matthew 15:4-6).

Jesus taught that He must be a priority even above one's family. He said, "Anyone who
loves his father or mother more than me is not worthy of me; anyone who loves his son or
daughter more than me is not worthy of me" (Matthew 10:37).

Jesus honored and respected His parents by obeying them while He grew up and providing
for His mother's care once He was gone (Luke 2:51; John 19:26, 27).

The Hebrew word *kabed* means to make honorable or to glorify. This verb has a wide range of
connotations that far exceeds simple obedience. It is important to obey parents, but children
must also show their parents respect. The Bible strictly warns children against cursing and
abusing their parents (Exodus 21:15-17).

On the other hand, Jesus clearly pointed out that God must be the priority. God's will is more
important than the will of one's parents (Judges 14:1-4; Matthew 10:37; Luke 13:15, 16). When parents
command or model something that is against God's will or clearly goes against loving God and
neighbor, they can still be honored without being obeyed.

# 6

# DO NOT MURDER

## THOU SHALT NOT KILL.

**PRINCIPLE**

## GOD CREATED HUMAN LIFE AND HOLDS IT SACRED.

**MEANING**

Murder is the unlawful killing of another human being, usually premeditated. The Hebrew word *ratsach,* always translated as "murder," is used for this commandment to contrast this prohibition with other forms of killing such as accidental death, war, self-defense, capital punishment, and the killing of animals. God created human beings in His own image. To take someone's life into one's own hands is to destroy the image of God.

**BIBLE EXAMPLES**

- After the flood, God instructed Noah and the generations to follow that death is the prescribed punishment for murder (Genesis 9:6).
- Cain, Simeon, Levi, Moses, Joab, King David, Absalom, and the Apostle Paul were all guilty of murder (Genesis 4:8; 35:25, 26; Exodus 2:11, 12; 2 Samuel 3:27; 11:14, 15; 13:28; Acts 9:1).
- The Bible says that God hates and detests hands that shed innocent blood (Proverbs 6:17).
- The Apostle Paul encouraged the believers in Rome to live at peace with everyone. He said that personal revenge belongs to God only (Romans 12:18, 19).
- The Apostle John wrote that anyone who hates his brother is a murderer. He also wrote that true love is evident in those who lay down their lives for others (1 John 3:15, 16).

**JESUS' TEACHINGS**

Jesus said, "You have heard that it was said to the people long ago, 'Do not murder, and anyone who murders will be subject to judgment.' But I tell you that anyone who is angry with his brother will be subject to judgment" (Matthew 5:21, 22).

Jesus said, "You have heard that it was said, 'Eye for eye, and tooth for tooth.' But I tell you, Do not resist an evil person. If someone strikes you on the right cheek, turn to him the other also" (Matthew 5: 38, 39).

Hearing the leaders of His day threatening to stone a woman to death, Jesus said, "If any one of you is without sin, let him be the first to throw a stone at her" (John 8:7).

**EXPLANATIONS**

Even though war, self-defense, and capital punishment are not prohibited by the sixth commandment, God values life and wants His people to preserve the lives of others and love their neighbors as themselves. This is an important factor of which to be mindful whenever the taking of the life of another human being is considered.

Jesus makes it clear that hatred for one's neighbor is the core cause for murder (Matthew 5:21, 22).
It is this same hatred that is forbidden by this commandment. As with the breaking of all other commandments, murder comes from the heart.

# 7 No Adultery

## THOU SHALT NOT COMMIT ADULTERY.

## GOD VALUES FAITHFULNESS AND SEXUAL PURITY.

Be faithful to one's husband or wife. Marriage vows made before God should be kept in spite of difficulties. Sex is a gift from God and is reserved for marriage only. Any sexually immoral act that betrays those vows, including premarital sex, is considered adultery. When we break the seventh commandment, we are sinning against God, our spouse, and against our own bodies (1 Corinthians 6:18).

- The Bible says that anyone who commits adultery should be put to death (Leviticus 20:10).
- God equates unfaithfulness to Him with adultery (Jeremiah 3:6-9).
- After King David committed adultery with Bathsheba, the prophet Nathan confronted him. David repented and wrote Psalm 51, a psalm of repentance. David wrote, "Create in me a pure heart, O God, and renew a steadfast spirit within me. Do not cast me from your presence or take your Holy Spirit from me" (Psalm 51:10, 11).
- Jesus forgave a woman who had been caught in adultery. Jesus told her that no one condemned her and to go and sin no more (John 8:10, 11).

Jesus said, "You have heard that it was said, 'Do not commit adultery.' But I tell you that anyone who looks at a woman lustfully has already committed adultery with her in his heart" (Matthew 5:27, 28).

Jesus also said, "I tell you that anyone who divorces his wife, except for marital unfaithfulness, and marries another woman commits adultery" (Matthew 19:9).

Jesus said, "…anyone who divorces his wife, except for marital unfaithfulness, causes her to become an adulteress, and anyone who marries the divorced woman commits adultery" (Matthew 5:31, 32).

Jewish law allowed a man to divorce his wife for any reason. Jesus' teachings shocked the disciples. They responded with: "If this is the situation between a husband and wife, it is better not to marry" (Matthew 19:10).

Paul taught that abandonment by an unbelieving spouse was also grounds for divorce (1 Corinthians 7:15).

Jesus said that the condition of the heart that leads to adultery is lust. The Apostle Paul wrote: "whatever is true, whatever is noble, whatever is right, whatever is pure, whatever is lovely, whatever is admirable—if anything is excellent or praiseworthy—think about such things" (Philippians 4:8).

# 8 DO NOT STEAL
## THOU SHALT NOT STEAL.

**PRINCIPLE**

# GOD VALUES PRODUCTIVITY, INTEGRITY, AND GENEROSITY.

**MEANING**

Respect other people's possessions. Stealing includes taking items that don't belong to us, defaulting on loans, not paying bills, cheating on tests, goofing off at work, cheating on income taxes, taking sick time when you or your dependents are not sick, stealing cable services, illegally downloading or copying software, music, movies, or printed material, and not giving to God.

**BIBLE EXAMPLES**

- The Apostle Paul wrote to the Ephesians telling them to stop stealing and to start working for their money, so that they could share with the needy (Ephesians 4:28).
- The Bible says that all people are to pay their taxes and repay their debts. The Scriptures warn against defaulting on loans and neglecting bills (Romans 13:6-8; Proverbs 22:26, 27).
- The prophet Malachi wrote that when people don't bring their full tithe and offering to God they are stealing directly from God. God promises to bless those who bring Him their full tithe and offering (Malachi 3:8-12).

**JESUS' TEACHINGS**

When we steal we don't trust God's provision. Jesus said "Therefore I tell you, do not worry about your life, what you will eat or drink; or about your body, what you will wear. Is not life more important than food, and the body more important than clothes? Look at the birds of the air; they do not sow or reap or store away in barns, and yet your heavenly Father feeds them. Are you not much more valuable than they?" (Matthew 6:25, 26).

Jesus said, "And if someone wants to sue you and take your tunic, let him have your cloak as well... Give to the one who asks you, and do not turn away from the one who wants to borrow from you" (Matthew 5:40, 42).

**EXPLANATIONS**

The Bible warns against taking out loans. The Bible also encourages those who do take out loans to repay their debt. Jesus encouraged those who loan money to forgive the debts of others. Jesus also encouraged people to give freely and allow others to borrow things from you without asking anything in return.

Jesus is presenting a picture of a caring kingdom, a kingdom where people give to others freely out of love. In Christ's kingdom, there would be no need for stealing out of lack of food, clothing, or shelter. In addition, there would be no need for loans or debt, because peoples' needs are cared for by one another. In fact, the early church expressed these principles in how they cared for each other (Acts 4:32-37).

# 9

# DO NOT LIE

## THOU SHALT NOT BEAR FALSE WITNESS AGAINST THY NEIGHBOUR.

## GOD IS TRUTH AND HE VALUES HONESTY.

Be trustworthy and maintain integrity by being honest. Lying can take the form of gossip, false accusations, blame, and self-deceit. It is important to keep promises and be responsible to the commitments we make. Liars cannot be trusted, and even when a liar tells the truth, he or she may not be believed. The Bible forbids attempting to deceive God.

- The Bible says that the wise keep all falsehoods and lies far from them (Proverbs 30:8).
- The Bible says that God hates a lying tongue, and delights in those who tell the truth (Proverbs 12:12).
- Those who speak the truth are valued by kings (Proverbs 16:13).
- In the early church, a man named Ananias and his wife Sapphira sold some property and claimed to donate the entire amount to the church. Instead, they kept some of the money for themselves. The Apostle Peter said they were free to keep some of the money, but since they claimed to bring the entire amount, they lied to the Holy Spirit. Their lie resulted in immediate death by the hand of God (Acts 5:1-11 ).

Jesus said, "The good man brings good things out of the good stored up in him, and the evil man brings evil things out of the evil stored up in him. But I tell you that men will have to give account on the day of judgment for every careless word they have spoken. For by your words you will be acquitted, and by your words you will be condemned" (Matthew 12:35-37).

Jesus said, "I am the way and the truth and the life. No one comes to the Father except through me" (John 14:6).

Before Joshua led the Israelites into the Promised Land, he sent spies into the city of Jericho. The prostitute Rahab housed the spies and helped them escape. When the authorities asked about the spies, Rahab deceived them and thereby saved the spies. Later, Rahab was saved because she honored God by preserving the lives of the spies. She knew God's will and His plans for the people of Israel; therefore she chose to obey the principles that honor God's will. Her decision to mislead and deceive her leaders as to the whereabouts of the Israelite spies was honored by God (Joshua 2:1-6; 6:17-25).

Truth-telling makes for a functional and just society. People who tell the truth can be trusted. Sensitive application of honesty and truth nurtures relationships and helps foster communities that are functional and enriching.

# 10 DO NOT COVET

## THOU SHALT NOT COVET THY NEIGHBOUR'S HOUSE... NOR ANY THING THAT IS THY NEIGHBOUR'S.

**PRINCIPLE**

## GOD VALUES HUMILITY, CONTENTMENT, AND PEACE.

**MEANING**

Be content with what we have. Don't long for things that belong to others. Avoid the pursuit of happiness and joy through the accumulation of material wealth, possessions, someone else's spouse, and other's friends. Don't allow earthly things to fill a void that only God can fill. Ask God to provide what we need. God promises that He will take care of our needs if we seek Him first and not money, popularity, or possessions.

**BIBLE EXAMPLES**

- King Saul was jealous of David's success and coveted the respect and praise David received from the women in all the towns (1 Samuel 18:6-9).
- King David coveted his neighbor Uriah's wife Bathsheba and he committed adultery with her. David then murdered Uriah to cover up his treachery (2 Samuel 11:1-27).
- The Apostle Paul encouraged the early church to be content with what they had and warned them about loving money and possessions. Paul said that the love of money is a root of all kinds of evil; it causes greed, envy, and pride (Philippians 4:11, 12; 1 Timothy 6:6-10; Hebrews 13:5).
- The Apostle John warned believers about loving the world and the things of the world. He said that anyone who loves the world does not have the love of God in him (1 John 2:15).

**JESUS' TEACHINGS**

Jesus said, "So do not worry, saying, 'What shall we eat?' or 'What shall we drink?' or 'What shall we wear?' For the pagans run after all these things, and your heavenly Father knows that you need them. But seek first his kingdom and his righteousness, and all these things will be given to you as well" (Matthew 6:31-33).

Jesus said, "A man's life does not consist in the abundance of his possessions" (Luke 12:15).

A rich young man with a lifelong commitment to keeping all the commandments came to Jesus and asked what more he needed to do. Jesus's response to the man's request for eternal life went right to the heart of the tenth commandment: "One thing you lack," he said. "Go, sell everything you have and give to the poor, and you will have treasure in heaven. Then come, follow me" (Mark 10:17-23).

**EXPLANATIONS**

Generally, the purpose of advertising and marketing is to feed on their customers' discontent by appealing to a person's selfish nature. These advertisers promise people fulfillment if they buy their product. Their ads seem to suggest that when you purchase a particular item, you will be surrounded by friends, a beautiful spouse, and a really great, enjoyable life. These advertisers know that people covet and that people have the tendency to be dissatisfied with what they have.

God wants us to be content with what we have and to keep our eyes focused on Him; not on things of this world (Philippians 4:11,12).

# WHICH IS THE MOST IMPORTANT COMMANDMENT?

**When the Pharisees asked Jesus which commandment in the law was the greatest, Jesus said, "'Love the Lord your God with all your heart and with all your soul and with all your mind.' This is the first and greatest commandment. And the second is like it: 'Love your neighbor as yourself.' All the Law and the Prophets hang on these two commandments" (Matthew 22:37-40).**

Every law is based on a principle. In Jesus' day, many people were obeying the law, but they weren't upholding God's principles. Jesus told the parable of the Good Samaritan to illustrate this concept. In this parable a man is attacked on a road and left for dead. As time passes, a priest and a Levite (someone who knows the law well) pass by the man and do not help him. Later, a Samaritan (considered to be a lower-class person) comes across the injured man and helps him; he even pays for his medical treatment. The law did not allow anyone to touch a dead body. Even though this man was not dead, he may have appeared to be dead to those passing by. The Samaritan risked disobeying the law in order to show mercy to an injured man. The priest and the Levite passed by the man for fear of breaking this law (Luke 10:25-37).

For Jesus, showing mercy to others and truly loving your neighbor is far more important than obeying a ceremonial purity law. Jesus encouraged people to live by the Spirit of the law rather than the letter of the law. He wanted people to make sure they understood *why* we obey a commandment. Paul wrote that with Christ the law is no longer written on tablets of stone, but it is written on our hearts. The reason we break a commandment stems from what is in our hearts. In the same way, the reason we obey a commandment is because our hearts have been transformed in Christ (2 Corinthians 3:1-17).

Today, people are to drive within a speed limit. Why? Because speeding is dangerous to ourselves and to other drivers and our lawmakers value life. For this reason, driving faster than the speed limit is against the law. However, when someone is rushing an injured friend or relative to the hospital, it is acceptable to set aside some traffic laws. In this situation, those who enforce laws accept the principle that life is more valuable than obeying the speed limit.

# Exodus 20:1-17

And God spoke all these words: "I am the Lord your God, who brought you out of Egypt, out of the land of slavery.

1   You shall have no other gods before me.

2   You shall not make for yourself an idol in the form of anything in heaven above or on the earth beneath or in the waters below. You shall not bow down to them or worship them; for I, the Lord your God, am a jealous God, punishing the children for the sin of the fathers to the third and fourth generation of those who hate me, but showing love to thousands who love me and keep my commandments.

3   You shall not misuse the name of the Lord your God, for the Lord will not hold anyone guiltless who misuses his name.

4   Remember the Sabbath day by keeping it holy. Six days you shall labor and do all your work, but the seventh day is a Sabbath to the Lord your God. On it you shall not do any work, neither you, nor your son or daughter, nor your manservant or maidservant, nor your animals, nor the alien within your gates. For in six days the Lord made the heavens and the earth, the sea, and all that is in them, but he rested on the seventh day. Therefore the Lord blessed the Sabbath day and made it holy.

5   Honor your father and your mother, so that you may live long in the land the Lord your God is giving you.

6   You shall not murder.

7   You shall not commit adultery.

8   You shall not steal.

9   You shall not give false testimony against your neighbor.

10  You shall not covet your neighbor's house. You shall not covet your neighbor's wife, or his manservant or maidservant, his ox or donkey, or anything that belongs to your neighbor." (NIV)

Contributor: Shawn Vander Lugt, MDiv

# The Lord's Prayer

Know God's Power & Forgiveness

Through the Seven Petitions

# Lord, Teach Us to Pray

Jesus' disciples had seen him pray many times. Sometimes he prayed all night and sometimes his prayers were just one sentence. But Jesus' followers made the connection between Jesus' intense prayer life and the power he showed in every aspect of life. They must have realized that prayer was the link. Finally, one disciple asked Jesus to teach them how to pray. Jesus gave them a deceptively simple, childlike prayer which has come to be known as "The Lord's Prayer." The prayer is recorded in Luke 11:2-4 and Matthew 6:9-13. Matthew's version highlights seven key parts:

> *Our Father in heaven,*
> *hallowed be your name,*
> *your kingdom come,*
> *your will be done on earth as it is in heaven.*
> *Give us today our daily bread.*
> *Forgive us our debts, as we also have forgiven our debtors.*
> *And lead us not into temptation, but deliver us from the evil one.*
>
> —Matthew 6:9-13

In this pattern, Jesus provided his followers with guidelines for prayer based on the attributes or characteristics of God.

The two main sections of the prayer divide with the words "your" and "our."

1. The first part centers on God, putting God in his rightful place in our priorities. Only by focusing on the patient and loving Father can we find the attitude that puts our own needs in perspective.

2. The second part focuses on our needs—body, soul, and spirit—and the needs of others. In just three brief requests, Jesus targets all of human behavior and character and reminds us that we always need him. It's been said that if these three requests are prayed properly, nothing more need be said. Only in moment-by-moment dependence on God will we experience the good things God wants to provide.

The Lord's Prayer is a dangerous, life-changing prayer. Jesus' enemies eventually killed him for asserting his close tie to God through addressing God as "Father." Until Jesus gave his followers the right to be called children of God, this would have been blasphemy.

Twenty-first-century Christians may take the privilege for granted, but the prayer is still a dangerous one: We do, in one sense, "take our lives in our hands" and offer them up again and again as sacrifice to the One who gave us all in the first place, receiving all of Life in return.

GOD'S ATTRIBUTE

WHAT DOES IT MEAN?

SCRIPTURE

APPLICATION

# *O*ur Father in heaven (NIV)
# *O*ur Father which art in heaven (KJV)

## GOD'S FATHERLY LOVE

God is a loving and compassionate Father who gives life, provides for and protects those who trust him. Like a caring human father, God wants a close relationship with his children. Addressing God as "Our Father" plunges the person praying into a relationship. A child approaching a loving father knows that father will give careful attention to the child's requests and will be lovingly inclined toward the child's best interests. The child knows the father will answer. This is how Jesus tells us to approach God—as trusting children of a patient, tender father.

*But to all who believed him [Jesus] and accepted him, he gave the right to become children of God. They are reborn—not with a physical birth resulting from human passion or plan, but a birth that comes from God.*
—John 1:12, 13 (New Living Translation)

*How great is the love the Father has lavished on us, that we should be called children of God!* —1 John 3:1

*Let us then approach the throne of grace with confidence, so that we may receive mercy and find grace to help us in our time of need.*
—Hebrews 4:16

During Jesus' time, people understood God to be awesome, majestic, and far away in the unreachable heavens. Though the Old Testament uses the metaphor of fatherhood when talking of God, no one would have dreamed of addressing God as "Father" in prayer. Jesus' use of the name "Abba" (like our "Daddy") must have stunned his disciples.

In fact, Jesus' use of the family name was so shocking to the religious leaders of his day that eventually he was accused of blasphemy and crucified for identifying himself as God's Son!

Jesus taught his followers that they should address God as "Father," and that their loving Father would care for all the needs of those who trust in him (see Matthew 7:7-11). Then, not only did Jesus encourage that relationship of trust, but he willingly died a horrible death to purchase the right of believers in Christ to be called children of God! It's hard to comprehend that the God who has all the power in the universe will listen to our prayers because of the actions of his Son, Jesus!

# *H*allowed be your name (NIV)
# *H*allowed be thy name (KJV)

## GOD'S HOLINESS

To hallow means to make holy. To "hallow" God's name means to honor it as holy and sacred. When we pray, we enter the presence of God with reverence, worship, and thanksgiving. We thank God not only for what he's done, but also for who he is. God's greatness and glory alone are worthy of praise and thankfulness. Thanksgiving recognizes that everything we have belongs to God, whether it be our talents, possessions, jobs, or children.

*Exalt the LORD our God and worship at his holy mountain, for the LORD our God is holy.* —Psalm 99:9

*You shall not misuse the name of the LORD your God, for the LORD will not hold anyone guiltless who misuses his name.* —Exodus 20:7

*So whether you eat or drink or whatever you do, do it all for the glory of God.* —1 Corinthians 10:31

*The earth is the Lord's, and everything in it, the world, and all who live in it.* —Psalm 24:1

Traditionally, God's people, the Jews, never said or wrote the name of God. To do so was considered not keeping the name of God holy. God's name represents his character, his plan, and his will. We often think of cursing as a common misuse of God's name, but what about attitudes of the heart? Lack of respect or indifference by one who professes love for God may be just as much a sin. Revelation 3:15, 16 shows God's attitude toward indifference: "I know your deeds, that you are neither cold nor hot. I wish you were either one or the other! So, because you are lukewarm—neither hot nor cold—I am about to spit you out of my mouth."

Jesus encouraged his followers to use God's name in honorable ways and for purposes that deepen and endear our bonds to him. Part of showing reverence for the holy name of God is thanking him for who he is and for what he's done. Many Psalms praise and worship God's holy name (see Psalms 100 and 148). Our greatest reverence, though, is shown by the stories our lives reveal. Our Father's name is most hallowed when we live in ways that attract others to him. (See 1 Corinthians 10:31; Matthew 5:16.)

# Your kingdom come (NIV)
# Thy kingdom come (KJV)

## GOD'S SOVEREIGNTY

God has supreme power and authority over everything in heaven and earth. When we acknowledge God's sovereignty, we affirm and welcome his reign in our lives. We promise to live in ways that honor him. But God's kingdom is both here and now—and yet to come. During Jesus' life on earth, his ministry was "to proclaim freedom for the prisoners, to recover sight for the blind, to release the oppressed, and to proclaim the year of the Lord's favor" (Luke 4:18, 19). When Jesus was around, people were freed from sickness, suffering, and pain. When Jesus returns to reign supreme, there will be no pain, suffering, or evil ever again. God will make everything right in the end.

*In the time of those kings, the God of heaven will set up a kingdom*
*that will never be destroyed, nor will it be left to another people.*
*It will crush all those kingdoms and bring them to an end, but it will itself endure forever.*
—Daniel 2:44

*And I heard a loud voice from the throne saying, "Now the dwelling of God is with men,*
*and he will live with them. They will be his people, and God himself will be with them*
*and be their God. He will wipe every tear from their eyes. There will be no more death or*
*mourning or crying or pain, for the old order of things has passed away."*
—Revelation 21:3, 4

Jesus said that the Kingdom of God was near (Mark 1:15). When asked when the Kingdom of God would come, Jesus said, "The kingdom of God does not come with your careful observation, nor will people say, 'Here it is,' or 'There it is,' because the kingdom of God is within you." God's kingdom will be evident in the lives of those who make him their Lord. This petition asks the Lord to change our lives so that his goodness is always evident through us. Some people have interpreted this prayer as an invitation to impact culture by passing laws calling people back to safer moral standards. But Jesus made clear his Church's mission: to lead people to himself. Jesus commissioned all disciples to proclaim that Jesus is King and Lord over all (Matthew 28:18-20). Our obedience to this commission helps spread God's kingdom throughout the world. This prayer can function as a petition for the strength and power we need to usher in God's kingdom on earth. When we focus on recognizing and embracing God's reign in this world, we help to make it visible.

# *Y*our will be done on earth as it is in heaven (NIV)
# *T*hy will be done in earth, as it is in heaven (KJV)

## GOD'S AUTHORITY

God's perfect will is always being done in heaven. But on earth, human free will results in selfishness, greed, and evil. In this part of the Lord's Prayer, we ask that God's will would take place on earth. More specifically, we pray for God's will to become our will. God calls each one of his children to live rightly and do good to others, caring for those around us as much as for ourselves. We pray that all people submit to the will of God over their own desires and faithfully love God and neighbors as themselves. Relationship with God depends on obedience to his will. God's will should be the context for everything we ask for, say, and do.

*Teach me to do your will, for you are my God;*
*may your good Spirit lead me on level ground.* —Psalm 143:10

*Not everyone who says to me, "Lord, Lord," will enter the kingdom of heaven,*
*but only he who does the will of my Father who is in heaven.*
*—Matthew 7:21*

*Jesus prayed for his Father's will: "Yet not as I will, but as you will."* —Matthew 26:39

*For whoever does the will of my Father in heaven is my brother and sister and mother.*
*—Matthew 12:50*

Philippians 2:3-8 says, "Do nothing out of selfish ambition or vain conceit, but in humility consider others better than yourselves." Our attitude should be like Jesus'. So often, when we come to God in prayer, we bring our own agendas. We want our will to be done, we want our wishes to be granted, and we want God to answer our prayers in a certain way. Often God's will differs from our own; in these situations, we need to trust God's will over our own desires.

For centuries, Christians have debated whether God's will is done whether or not we pray. Some question, "Why pray if God knows everything we need before we ask?"

Others have wondered whether God takes action at all if we don't initiate the request. While we trust in God's sovereignty and his ability to exercise his good will, we also trust his commands to exercise the muscles of our wills in prayer. We pray, believing in God's promises to respond in ways that are best for us (see Luke 18:1). Though we often pray for changes in circumstance, the real work of prayer changes us from the inside out (Romans 12:1, 2). The more we talk with God, the more we find ourselves wanting to please him. Prayer often changes our circumstances, but more importantly, it changes us and our priorities.

# *G*ive us this day our daily bread (NIV)
# *G*ive us this day our daily bread (KJV)

## GOD'S PROVIDENCE

God is able to provide for all our needs. The Greek word for "bread" represents not just food, but every physical thing we need. When we pray for our daily bread, we ask God to provide for our material, physical, emotional, relational, and spiritual needs for that day. Daily bread can include the daily needs of ministries, people, communities, leaders, family, friends, as well as personal needs. God commits himself to provide for his children, yet God knows more about what we need than we ourselves know. By praying for daily bread, we are not taking it for granted, but acknowledging that all our life depends on his mercy.

*But seek first his kingdom and his righteousness, and all these things will be given to you as well. Therefore do not worry about tomorrow, for tomorrow will worry about itself. Each day has enough trouble of its own. —Matthew 6:33, 34*

*Then Jesus declared, "I am the bread of life. He who comes to me will never go hungry, and he who believes in me will never be thirsty." —John 6:35*

*Every good and perfect gift is from above, coming down from the Father of the heavenly lights, who does not change like shifting shadows. —James 1:17*

The phrase "this day" shows that we rely on God one day at a time. Compared to the rest of people on earth, we are wealthy Christians. It's far too easy for us to forget that not only our talents, resources, and opportunities come from God, but also the next meal. Asking for what we need each day—even if it's already in our refrigerators—encourages a relationship with the One who gives all. He wants us to remember and ask for his help with the most basic needs: disciplining our children, speaking to a spouse, growing spiritually, resolving a conflict with a

friend, reuniting with family members, leading ministries, conducting an office meeting, and going to the movies.

So what if we ask for the wrong things—things that, while they may be good in themselves are not in God's plan for us? As a loving Father, God will always give us what's best for us, not necessarily what we want. What we receive will be what's right for us and fits God's greater goal of transforming us to be more like him.

*F*orgive us our debts,
   as we also have forgiven our debtors (NIV)
*A*nd forgive us our debts, as we forgive our debtors (KJV)

# GOD'S MERCY

We ask God to forgive the wrong we have done as well as our neglect of the good things we should have done. But there is a catch: God will forgive us only as much as we forgive those who have injured us. God is merciful and he expects us to be also. If we refuse to forgive others, how can we expect God's forgiveness?

### Debts vs. Trespasses

Several Greek words are used to describe sin. The Lord's prayer in the Gospel of Matthew uses the word *ophelema* which is rendered "debt" (Matthew 6:12). However, only two verses later, the gospel uses the word *paraptoma*, which is usually rendered "trespass" (Matthew 6:14). In all these cases, sin is what separates us from God, our friends, and our family. Without forgiveness—whether it be forgiving debts or forgiving trespasses—relationships suffer and redemption is not possible.

*If we confess our sins, he is faithful and just and will forgive us our sins and purify us from all unrighteousness.* —1 John 1:9

*For as high as the heavens are above the earth, so great is his love for those who fear him; as far as the east is from the west, so far has he removed our transgressions from us.* —Psalm 103:12, 13

*No longer will a man teach his neighbor, or a man his brother, saying, "Know the Lord," because they will all know me, from the least of them to the greatest. For I will forgive their wickedness and will remember their sins no more.* —Hebrews 8:11, 12

The New Testament uses five Greek words to talk about sin. The meanings range from slipping and falling (unintentional), "missing the mark" as an arrow misses the target, stepping across the line (intentional), "lawlessness" or open rebellion against God, and the word used in Matthew 6:12, which refers to a spiritual debt to God. This last aspect of sin is what Jesus illustrates in the following story:

Jesus told a parable about a man who owed the king over one million dollars. After the man begged for mercy, the king forgave the debt. Afterward, that same man demanded a few dollars from his neighbor. When his neighbor could not pay, the man had him thrown into prison. Once the king heard about it, he had the man turned over to the jailers until he could repay the debt. Jesus finished by saying, "This is how my heavenly Father will treat each of you unless you forgive your brother from your heart" (Matthew 18:23-35). Jesus makes it clear that God will not show mercy to the merciless!

Sometimes we are unaware of our sins. Therefore, praying for forgiveness requires listening quietly in God's presence so that he may reveal to us our own acts of disobedience, our resentments, and our unresolved issues. Though as Christians we inevitably continue to sin, our lives ought to be characterized by a decreasing frequency of sin and an increased sensitivity to it.

*A*nd lead us not into temptation,
but deliver us from the evil one (NIV)
*A*nd lead us not into temptation, but deliver us from evil (KJV)

# GOD'S PROTECTION

We are taught to pray that we won't be tempted to do wrong. In a practical way, this is like praying that God will keep our minds off of tempting situations. People used to excuse bad behavior by saying, "The devil made me do it." But in reality, the devil cannot make us do wrong. We do it ourselves. God won't make us obey him, but he does give us the power to walk away from wrong choices. The Holy Spirit gives us strength to withstand temptation, avoid sin, and strive for holiness. Satan is constantly seeking to attack the hearts and minds of those who love God. God provides us with the defenses we need to protect ourselves against the weapons of Satan. By praying for protection, we prepare each day for battle against evil.

*No temptation has seized you except what is common to man. And God is faithful; he will not let you be tempted beyond what you can bear. But when you are tempted, he will also provide a way out so that you can stand up under it.* —1 Corinthians 10:13

*Therefore put on the full armor of God, so that when the day of evil comes, you may be able to stand your ground.* —Ephesians 6:10-13a

*In this you greatly rejoice, though now for a little while you may have had to suffer grief in all kinds of trials. These have come so that your faith—of greater worth than gold, which perishes even though refined by fire—may be proved genuine and may result in praise, glory and honor when Jesus Christ is revealed.* —1 Peter 1:6, 7

The Greek word for "temptation" emphasizes the idea of testing or proving, rather than simply an enticement to sin. The Bible is clear that God is good and holy, and he would never lead us into sin. James 1:13, 14 says that God does not tempt anyone, but each person is tempted by his own evil desire. So why do we pray this petition? Because it's better to avoid danger and all the trouble caused by sin than to have to fight and face the possibility of losing to it! Realistically, having the potential to do evil is part of being a human being—it gives us the opportunity to show what we are becoming. Genuine freedom requires that there be a choice between good and evil.

Yet, we also know that trials strengthen faith and character (1 Peter 1:6, 7). Through our trials, we are driven closer to God through prayer and Scripture. We are reminded not to place our trust in ourselves. Through trials, we learn to trust God more, and we gain the ability to help others in similar trials. So while human nature resists the realities of trials and temptations, the maturing Christian accepts the refining process they bring. All that's left is to throw ourselves on the Father who has promised not to leave us unprotected and exposed to attacks from the enemy (Satan), but to protect, deliver, and forgive.

# REASONS TO FORGIVE

| Reason | Result | Bible Passage |
|---|---|---|
| Forgiveness is characteristic of a Christian life. | By loving our enemies, we show that we are children of God. | Blessed are the merciful, for they will be shown mercy. —Matthew 5:7 |
| | When a Christian refuses to forgive, that person puts himself above God as judge. | You have heard that it was said, "Love your neighbor and hate your enemy." But I tell you: Love your enemies and pray for those who persecute you, that you may be sons of your Father in heaven. He causes his sun to rise on the evil and the good, and sends rain on the righteous and the unrighteous. —Matthew 5:43-45 |
| We follow Jesus, our role model, who forgave. | Only through Jesus are we forgiven and made right with God. | Be kind and compassionate to one another, forgiving each other, just as in Christ God forgave you. —Ephesians 4:32 |
| | Whatever we may suffer cannot come close to the offenses Jesus Christ forgave during his time on earth. | Whoever claims to live in him must walk as Jesus did. —1 John 2:6 Jesus said, "Father, forgive them, for they do not know what they are doing." —Luke 23:34 |
| We are made in the image of God, who forgives. | We reflect the beauty and glory of our Creator when we forgive. | A man's wisdom gives him patience; it is to his glory to overlook an offense. —Proverbs 19:11 |
| Forgiveness keeps Satan from gaining a foothold. | Forgiveness frees the conscience of guilt and brings peace of mind. | If you forgive anyone, I also forgive him. And what I have forgiven— if there was anything to forgive— I have forgiven in the sight of Christ for your sake, in order that Satan might not outwit us. For we are not unaware of his schemes. —2 Corinthians 2:10, 11 |
| Christ's Body, the Church, cannot function without forgiveness. | Grudges and resentments tarnish the Church's witness and prevent the full benefits of God's gifts. | Therefore, if you are offering your gift at the altar and there remember that your brother has something against you, leave your gift there in front of the altar. First go and be reconciled to your brother; then come and offer your gift. —Matthew 5:23, 24 |
| Only by forgiving others can we expect our own prayers for forgiveness to be answered. | God will treat us in the same way we treat others. | For if you forgive men when they sin against you, your heavenly Father will also forgive you. But if you do not forgive men their sins, your Father will not forgive your sins. —Matthew 6:14, 15 |

# OTHER VERSES ON PRAYER

### Abide in Christ

*If you remain in me and my words remain in you, ask whatever you wish, and it will be given you.* —John 15:7

### Ask, Seek and Knock

*Ask and it will be given to you; seek and you will find; knock and the door will be opened to you. For everyone who asks receives; he who seeks finds; and to him who knocks, the door will be opened.* —Matthew 7:7, 8

### Do Not Be Anxious

*Do not be anxious about anything, but in everything, by prayer and petition, with thanksgiving, present your requests to God. And the peace of God, which transcends all understanding, will guard your hearts and your minds in Christ Jesus.* —Philippians 4:6, 7

### Pray Continually

*Be joyful always; pray continually; give thanks in all circumstances, for this is God's will for you in Christ Jesus.* —1 Thessalonians 5:16-18

### God Knows What We Need

*In the same way, the Spirit helps us in our weakness. We do not know what we ought to pray for, but the Spirit himself intercedes for us with groans that words cannot express. And he who searches our hearts knows the mind of the Spirit, because the Spirit intercedes for the saints in accordance with God's will.* —Romans 8:26, 27

### Prayer Is Effective

*Is any one of you in trouble? He should pray. Is anyone happy? Let him sing songs of praise. Is any one of you sick? He should call the elders of the church to pray over him and anoint him with oil in the name of the Lord. And the prayer offered in faith will make the sick person well; the Lord will raise him up. If he has sinned, he will be forgiven. Therefore confess your sins to each other and pray for each other so that you may be healed. The prayer of a righteous man is powerful and effective.* —James 5:13-16

# HOW CAN I PRAY?

How can I pray "**our**" if I live only for myself?

How can I pray "**Father**" if I do not act like his child?

How can I pray "**who art in heaven**" if I am laying up no treasure there?

How can I pray "**hallowed be Thy name**" if I don't care about being holy myself?

How can I pray "**Thy kingdom come**" if I live for *my* kingdom, power, and wealth?

How can I pray "**Thy will be done**" if I disobey his Word?

How can I pray "**on earth as it is in heaven**" if I will not serve him here and now?

How can I pray "**give us ... our daily bread**" if I am dishonest or unwilling to share what I have with others?

How can I pray "**forgive us our debts**" if I nurture resentment against another?

How can I pray "**lead us not into temptation**" if I willingly place myself in its path?

How can I pray "**deliver us from evil**" if I refuse to put on all of God's armor?

How can I pray "**Thine is the kingdom**" if my life does not reflect his lordship?

How can I pray "**Thine is the ... power**" if I fear what people may do?

How can I pray "**Thine is the ... glory**" if I seek honor for myself?

How can I pray "**forever**" if my life is bounded only by the things of time?

# THE LORD'S PRAYER

Rather than giving us a formula to repeat over and over, Jesus gave us a model prayer illustrating first of all what our relationship with God should be like (the total dependence of children on a loving Father), and also the three main purposes of prayer:

- To declare God's holiness
- To usher in God's kingdom
- To do God's will

Seven distinct parts emphasize seven of God's attributes that help to place all of our needs and desires in proper perspective.

| GOD'S ATTRIBUTE | FOCUS | PETITION |
|---|---|---|
| God's Love | God is a loving Father | *Our Father in heaven* |
| God's Holiness | God's name is holy | *Hallowed be your name* |
| God's Sovereignty | There is no one above God | *Your kingdom come* |
| God's Authority | God has the supreme authority | *Your will be done on earth as it is in heaven* |
| God's Providence | God is the source of everything we need | *Give us today our daily bread* |
| God's Mercy | Forgiveness is our greatest need | *Forgive us our debts, as we also have forgiven our debtors* |
| God's Protection | Trials prove our faith and develop our characters | *And lead us not into temptation, but deliver us from the evil one* |

Contributor: Shawn Vander Lugt, M.Div.

# The Beatitudes

What Are the Beatitudes?
How Do They Relate to Us Today?

# WHAT ARE THE
# BEATITUDES?

The word *beatitude* comes from a Latin word (*beatus*) that means "happy" or "blessed." So the word beatitude is about some happiness or blessedness. What does it mean to be happy or blessed? The answer to this question is found in the context of the Beatitudes in Matthew 5.

The Beatitudes are the first part of Jesus' teachings called the Sermon on the Mount, (Matthew 5:1–7:29). In Matthew 4:17 Jesus began his ministry by announcing the coming of the kingdom of heaven: "Repent, for the kingdom of heaven is near." In Matthew 4:23–25, Jesus healed the sick throughout Galilee. This healing was a demonstration of the coming kingdom of heaven, of the fulfillment of God's promises through his prophets in the Old Testament. The teachings in the Sermon on the Mount, then, are descriptions and instructions for those living in the kingdom of heaven.

The Beatitudes are not imperatives; they are not commands the believer must fulfill to enter the kingdom of God. Rather, they are results of the coming of this kingdom. They are part of the Gospel, the good news that Jesus, the Messiah, has come. The good news is that God was about to intervene decisively in history and produce people like the ones described in the Sermon on the Mount.

 **Kingdom of God/Heaven**

The expression "kingdom of heaven" only occurs in the Gospel according to Matthew. Why? Because the Gospel of Matthew appears to have been for a Jewish audience, Matthew avoids using the name of God—out of respect, Jews avoid pronouncing God's name.

- The idea of the kingdom uses an important metaphor in the Old Testament: God is King (Psalm 47:7). Kings in the ancient world had absolute power over their dominions. However, they also had responsibilities toward their subjects. Kings were supposed to:

    - *Provide protection for their territories and the people in them*
    - *Provide for the needs of their subjects*
    - *Maintain order in the kingdom, especially legal order*
    - *Represent the deity (in the Old Testament, God)—the king stood for God, representing his authority to the people*

# BLESSED ARE THE POOR IN SPIRIT, FOR THEIRS IS THE KINGDOM OF HEAVEN.

## MEANING
—Matthew 5:3

The "poor in spirit" are those who recognize their need for God in all things. Like the poor and destitute who depend on others, the poor in spirit know that only God can save and protect them.

| What the WORLD Says | What JESUS Says |
|---|---|
| The world and every kind of human-made religion value the "spiritual master," the guru, the great teacher. The idea is that if you know and do the right things, you can find your own spiritual salvation. People have their own answers to their problems, if they could only recognize it. | Jesus tells us that the opposite is true. The truly happy people are those who have recognized they are spiritually bankrupt before God. Their happiness consists in relying on God's strength because they know he cannot fail, and having the certainty that in the kingdom of God, the Messiah will be fully in charge (Isaiah 29:19). |

## RELATED TEXTS

"Once more the humble will rejoice in the LORD…" (Isaiah 29:19). See also: Luke 6:20; Matthew 18:4; Isaiah 61:1.

## QUESTIONS

In what areas of your life are you trying to make it on your own, instead of asking God for help?

### Now and Future Kingdom

• In the New Testament, the kingdom of heaven is God's gracious rule. In other words, it is where God's will is done. The gospels make it clear that the kingdom was a present experience (Luke 11:20, 17:21). Jesus' miracles, teachings, and ministry are all manifestations of the kingdom.

• Yet, the rest of the New Testament, the apostolic letters, makes it also clear that the kingdom is a reality in the future. That is, the fullness of the kingdom will only be experienced when Jesus comes back at the end of times.

• Some theologians call these two realities about the kingdom of heaven the "already-not yet." The kingdom of heaven and the promises within it are *already* part of the church's experience. However, the fullness of the kingdom's power and influence is *not yet* experienced. Christ will bring about the fullness of the kingdom in his second coming.

# BLESSED ARE THOSE WHO MOURN, FOR THEY WILL BE COMFORTED.

—Matthew 5:4

## MEANING

"Those who mourn" refers to people wishing God to send his Messiah, hoping God will restore his kingdom and set the world right. Isaiah 61:2–3 tells of the coming Messiah who will "comfort all who mourn, and provide for those who grieve in Zion". These are people who understand the mess the world is in and wish for God's redemption. Their comfort consists in knowing that the Messiah has come and the redemption they have hoped for is about to occur!

| What the WORLD Says | What JESUS Says |
| --- | --- |
| Today we avoid grief and pain. "How can a mournful person be happy?" The pursuit of happiness has become for us a goal above all goals. We have become very adept to hiding from pain and reality. Nothing is solved, but we can continue to pretend to be happy. | In stark contrast, Jesus asserts that the way to true happiness must come through a radical shift in thought, a change of mind that first makes us see ourselves as we really are—and our world as it really is—and mourn. Only after we recognize this sorrow can God comfort us. Knowing that the Messiah has come and offers redemption is the greatest comfort for those who mourn. |

## RELATED TEXTS

"As a mother comforts her child, so will I comfort you…" (Isaiah 66:13).

"Do not let your hearts be troubled. Trust in God; trust also in me" (John 14:1).

"I tell you the truth, you will weep and mourn while the world rejoices. You will grieve, but your grief will turn to joy" (John 16:20).

"For the Lamb at the center of the throne will be their shepherd; he will lead them to springs of living water. And God will wipe away every tear from their eyes" (Revelation 7:17).

See also: Isaiah 61:2; John 16:7.

## QUESTIONS

Ask God to show you things in your life to which you may be insensitive. Remember that the Lord will always be with you, comforting you through this painful process. If there are areas in your life that need changing, ask God to redeem them.

# BLESSED ARE THE MEEK, FOR THEY WILL INHERIT THE EARTH.

—Matthew 5:5

## MEANING

This beatitude alludes to Psalm 37:11: "But the meek will inherit the land…." The Psalm is comparing the "evil" and "wicked" with the meek. In fact, Psalm 37:3, 5 seem to define what the psalmist means by the meek, "Trust in the LORD and do good…. Commit your way to the LORD; trust in him…." The prophet Zephaniah uses the same expression during a prophetic oracle of judgment: "…because I will remove from this city those who rejoice in their pride… But I will leave within you the meek and humble, who trust in the name of the LORD" (Zephaniah 3:11–12).

In addition, the word *meek* is an important adjective in the Bible. It is used to describe Moses in Numbers 12:3, and usually translated as "humble." Jesus describes himself with the same word in Matthew 11:29, "…for I am gentle and humble in heart…." The third Beatitude, then, refers to the meekness necessary to trust in God. It also refers to the attitude of God's servant: the meekness to serve God and do his will above our own.

| What the WORLD Says | What JESUS Says |
| --- | --- |
| It is the proud and strong who will inherit the earth. Only the mighty have the power to seize the prize of ruling the planet. Only those who are clever and confident in themselves and their abilities have any hope of holding on to authority and dominion. "Nice guys finish last" describes this attitude that gentleness never gets you anywhere. | Although it may appear that meekness is a disadvantage according to the values of this world, it is a wonderful thing in the values of God. It is God's invitation to trust in him, to have the certainty that his plans and work will accomplish what he promised. |

Old Testament prophets communicated God's promise to restore the land to Israel. This promise was taken to be limited to the land that God originally promised to Abraham. But in the New Testament, the promise is extended. It is a promise for "a new heaven and a new earth" (Revelation 21:1, 2 Peter 3:13). It is the new heaven and new earth that the meek will inherit.

## QUESTIONS

What areas of your life hinder you from obeying or accepting God's will? Pray that God will help you accept his will with meekness.

## RELATED TEXTS

"For the Lord takes delight in his people; he crowns the humble with salvation" (Psalm 149:4).

See also: Psalm 37:3, 5, 11; 72:4; Isaiah 61:1; Numbers 12:3.

### Old Testament Beatitudes

There are many beatitudes that occur in the Old Testament, some of which sound remarkably similar to Jesus' words.

- Psalm 41:1 says, "Blessed is he who has regard for the weak…" and we remember Jesus' beatitude about the merciful (Matthew 5:7).

- The book of Psalms opens with a blessing on righteous behavior: Jesus tells us that those who hunger and thirst for this righteousness shall be satisfied (Matthew 5:6).

- Psalm 32:1–2 presents a beatitude upon all whom the Lord has forgiven. The psalm goes on to speak of what it is like to confess utter dependence upon God. Jesus speaks of those who are poor in spirit as being blessed inheritors of the Kingdom of God.

- In Proverbs 8:34–35, personified wisdom says, "Blessed is the man who listens to me… for he who finds me finds life." Jesus ends the Sermon on the Mount by advising his hearers to take his words to heart. Then he reveals to them the consequences—it is a matter of life and death (Matthew 7:24–27).

# BLESSED ARE THOSE WHO HUNGER AND THIRST FOR RIGHTEOUSNESS FOR THEY WILL BE FILLED.

—Matthew 5:6

## MEANING

Just as poverty leads to hunger, the recognition of one's spiritual poverty leads to a hunger for righteousness. Jesus is talking to people who desire God's rule. It is a rule that brings justice for all. It is a reign in which God will satisfy the hungry and thirsty for righteousness. A fulfillment of God's promise in Isaiah 65:13, "My servants will eat...my servants will rejoice...."

| What the WORLD Says | What JESUS Says |
| --- | --- |
| Hungering for things to be right is a fool's game. Nothing ever changes. It's fine to compromise and to set aside honor when doing what is right is inconvenient. It's all politics, so quit worrying about what is right, just go for what you need. You gotta look out for number one! | Jesus holds out the promise that those who are starved for righteousness will be satisfied. His kingdom is characterized by "righteousness, peace and joy in the Holy Spirit" (Romans 14:17). |

## RELATED TEXTS

"If anyone is thirsty, let him come to me and drink..." (John 7:37).
See also: Isaiah 55:1–13; 65:13; John 6:48; Romans 14:17.

### Blessings and Curses

Luke's gospel also contains a series of "woes" which are the opposites of the blessings (Luke 6:24–26).

- The woes describe the natural consequences to ignoring God's will. They tell us what we can expect if we do not live the way God desires.

- Here the blessings and curses are parallel, much the same as in Deuteronomy 28:1–19. At Mount Sinai, Moses set the covenant between God and the Israelites, laying out the natural consequences (both the blessings and the curses) of the people's responses.

- The parallel structure of the two passages gives the sermon in Luke's account the same authoritative feel of Moses' utterance. Jesus lays out its principles before his disciples and asks them the question, "Why do you call me, 'Lord, Lord,' and do not do what I say?" (Luke 6:46).

- It is clear Jesus claims authority for this teaching, and the Gospel of Matthew records the shock his hearers felt when faced with such claims (Matthew 7:28-29).

## QUESTIONS

In what ways has God satisfied you when you have hungered and thirsted for righteousness?

# BLESSED ARE THE MERCIFUL, FOR THEY WILL BE SHOWN MERCY.

—Matthew 5:7

## MEANING

Mercy is part of God's own nature. "The LORD, the LORD, the compassionate and gracious God, slow to anger, abounding in love and faithfulness…." (Exodus 34:6). Besides, God expects mercy from his people: "He has shown you, O man, what is good. And what does the LORD require of you? To act justly and to love mercy and to walk humbly with your God" (Micah 6:8). People who have experienced mercy and forgiveness are filled with gratitude. Their gratitude cultivates a merciful attitude in return.

| What the WORLD Says | What JESUS Says |
|---|---|
| "We want justice!" "Take no prisoners" are the slogans of the proud, the strong and the careless. We like to condemn others to make ourselves feel better. Our world idolizes the arrogant and merciless in the sports world, the world of wealth and fame, and on the movie screen. "We are the champions—no time for losers." Mercy has become a liability—it is way too costly and will prevent the attainment of our goals. | Jesus again challenges the way the rest of the world thinks. Jesus lifts up mercy as an essential quality. In fact, mercy is what Jesus' life was all about—God's mercy to us. In many places Jesus makes the connection between giving mercy and receiving it (See Matthew 6:12–15, 18:21–35). It is not that we can buy God's mercy by our own acts of mercy, but that only those who know God's mercy can be truly merciful and receive God's most precious gift—eternal life. |

## RELATED TEXTS

"But you, O Lord, are a compassionate and gracious God…" (Psalm 86:15).

"…Return to the LORD your God, for he is gracious and compassionate, slow to anger and abounding in love…" (Joel 2:13).

See also: Psalm 103:8, 145:8; Luke 6:36.

## QUESTIONS

Which people in your life do you find it most difficult to be merciful to? In what practical ways can you demonstrate God's mercy in your local community?

# BLESSED ARE THE PURE IN HEART FOR THEY WILL SEE GOD.

—Matthew 5:8

## MEANING

Seeing God is one of the greatest hopes of the believer (1 John 3:2–3). But only the pure in heart may receive this blessing. Purity of heart, the heart that desires only what God wants, is not the result of personal effort. In other words, a pure heart is not the same as maturity of Christian experience. A pure heart is clean of sin. Only Christ can clean us from sin. God must give a pure heart (Psalm 51:10). Although purity of heart is not something we work toward, it is something we desire and God grants.

| What the WORLD Says | What JESUS Says |
|---|---|
| While our culture values things like pure air, pure water, pure food, it seems to devalue the pure heart. Some people insist on a "smoke-free" environment but do not mind a polluted heart. | True happiness begins in the presence of God. It is a hope that sustains and inspires those living in the kingdom of heaven. One of Jesus' constant criticisms of the Jewish leaders was their hypocrisy. That is, their desire to appear pure and holy, while being corrupted and impure inside. Jesus came to fulfill the promise in Ezekiel 36:25–27: "I will sprinkle clean water on you, and you will be clean… I will give you a new heart and put a new spirit in you…." |

## RELATED TEXTS

"Create in me a pure heart, O God…" (Psalm 51:10).

"…But we know that when he appears, we shall be like him, for we shall see him as he is. Everyone who has this hope in him purifies himself, just as he is pure" (1 John 3:2–3).

See also: Exodus 33:20; Psalm 24:3–4; Psalm 51; Hebrews 12:14; Revelation 22:1–4.

## QUESTIONS

What might happen if you pray to the Lord as David did in Psalm 51, verse 10: "Create in me a pure heart, O God, and renew a steadfast spirit within me"?

# BLESSED ARE THE PEACEMAKERS FOR THEY WILL BE CALLED SONS OF GOD.

—Matthew 5:9

## MEANING

This Beatitude brings together two important Old Testament concepts: peace and sons of God. Peace is a central characteristic of the kingdom of heaven. "The wolf will live with the lamb, the leopard will lie down with the goat, the calf and the lion and the yearling together, and a little child will lead them…" (Isaiah 11:6). Those who would normally be at war with each other will be in harmony. All things are made right and peace prevails. The Old Testament applies the title of "son of God" to the Messiah (Psalm 2:7). However, in the New Testament, the Apostle Paul explains that when we are in Christ, we "receive the full rights of sons;" in other words, we are made adopted children of God (Galatians 4:5).

| What the WORLD Says | What JESUS Says |
|---|---|
| Peace at any price, Give peace a chance. Peace—the cessation of all conflict—has become what a world in war is desperately looking for. Some feel world peace would solve all problems; others are ready to buy peace at almost any cost. Many seek a personal peace through a variety of avenues—drugs, music, meditation, and others. Still, the cessation of conflict will not substitute for true peace, the kind of peace Jesus offers. | Jesus, before leaving this earth, promised his disciples his peace: "Peace I leave with you; my peace I give you. I do not give to you as the world gives…" (John 14:27). His peace is a clear sign that the kingdom is in our midst. Only Jesus makes this peace possible (Ephesians 2:14) and only in him we become adopted children (Galatians 4:5). |

## RELATED TEXTS

"If it is possible, as far as it depends on you, live at peace with everyone" (Romans 12:18).

See also: Psalm 4:8; Isaiah 9:6; Romans 5:1.

*See "Shalom" on pages 84 and 85.*

## QUESTIONS

Can you think of a difficult or painful time in your life when you experienced Jesus' peace in a special way? How is the peace that Jesus gives different from the kind of peace the world promises?

# BLESSED ARE THOSE WHO ARE PERSECUTED BECAUSE OF RIGHTEOUSNESS, FOR THEIRS IS THE KINGDOM OF HEAVEN.

—Matthew 5:10

## MEANING

Just like the kingdom of heaven belongs to the poor in spirit, it also belongs to the ones persecuted because of righteousness. This verse is a reminder of God's prophets in the Old Testament. These were people who stood in for the right. They encountered opposition; they were mocked and harmed because they stood for what was right. But their reward is great. They truly enjoy the benefits of the kingdom of heaven.

| What the WORLD Says | What JESUS Says |
| --- | --- |
| Principles are good, but not if they get you killed or cause you grief. Righteousness has little foundation in our world today. Standards for right and wrong are not defined by what God desires for our good. People get away with what they can. | Jesus made it clear to his disciples that persecution would occur: "If they persecuted me, they will persecute you also" (John 15:20). Often doing what is right leads people to feel lonely, isolated, and persecuted. However, Jesus promised that he would not leave these people alone. He sent the Holy Spirit to guide and comfort. Besides, he also promises that "Now is your time of grief, but I will see you again and you will rejoice, and no one will take away your joy" (John 16:22). |

## RELATED TEXTS

"And the God of all grace, who called you to his eternal glory in Christ, after you have suffered a little while, will himself restore you and make you strong, firm and steadfast" (1 Peter 5:10).

"But even if you should suffer for what is right, you are blessed... But in your hearts set apart Christ as Lord..." (1 Peter 3:14–15).

See also: Luke 6:22–23; John 15:18–21.

## QUESTIONS

Think of a time when you felt like speaking up for what was right. If you did not speak up, what prevented you from doing so? If you did, what resulted from it? How can you help others who are facing persecution because of righteousness?

# BLESSED ARE THOSE WHO HAVE NOT SEEN YET HAVE BELIEVED.

—John 20:29

## MEANING

Jesus is speaking about his resurrection. It is one thing to have seen the risen Christ as hundreds of his disciples did (1 Corinthians 15:6) and yet another to believe today based on the word of these eyewitnesses. There is a special blessing experienced by those who know that Christ has risen, based on the testimony alone.

| What the WORLD Says | What JESUS Says |
| --- | --- |
| "Who really knows what happened back there 2000 years ago?" "People don't just get up from the dead. The whole thing was probably a hoax or a mistake." There is much skepticism about the events that eyewitness recorded in the Bible. | "I am the resurrection and the life" (John 11:25). We have the testimony of the Apostles (1 Corinthians 15:3-8), and the ministry of the Holy Spirit (John 15:26). |

## RELATED TEXTS

"Though you have not seen him, you love him; and even though you do not see him now, you believe in him and are filled with an inexpressible and glorious joy…" (1 Peter 1:8).

See also: John 1:12, 17:20–21; 1 Corinthians 15.

## QUESTIONS

When have you seen God give the gift of faith to yourself or other believers?

 ## Shalom

Traditionally, this Hebrew word is translated as "peace." When we think about peace, we tend to define it as absence of conflict. However, *shalom* means much more than that.

- The best example of what *shalom* means is the Garden of Eden. In Eden, all things functioned according to the order and purpose that God assigned them. There was order and harmony, balance and wholeness.
- When Adam and Eve rebelled against God, this state of being was broken. Things are no longer the way they are supposed to be.

# IT is MORE BLESSED TO GIVE THAN TO RECEIVE.

—Acts 20:35

## MEANING

Giving, especially to those who are in need, will lead to happiness quicker than if we are only on the receiving end. The life that constantly takes without giving is a selfish life, and selfishness only leads to greater unhappiness. Meeting other peoples' needs is the road to a blessed life.

| What the WORLD Says | What JESUS Says |
| --- | --- |
| "Get what you can now—after all, the one who dies with the most toys wins." No one's going to take care of you. If you're generous, you'll be taken advantage of. You have to make it on your own. Besides, you can't please everyone, so you have to please yourself. Charity is a scam, so get what you can, and take what you can get. | Jesus tells us that he came to serve, not to be served (Matthew 20:28). He came to give himself and calls us to the same lifestyle. It is easy to miss that this giving was a joy to him because he delighted to do what God had called him to (John 17:13). "A servant is not greater than his master" and we are blessed when we follow the Master's example (John 13:15–17). |

## RELATED TEXTS

"…And if you spend yourselves in behalf of the hungry and satisfy the needs of the oppressed, then your light will rise in the darkness, and your night will become like the noonday" (Isaiah 58:10). See also: Matthew 6:1–4; Luke 6:38; 22:24–30.

- *Shalom* is about relationships. When humans sinned in the Garden, three relationships were broken:
  1. *Our relationship with God;*
  2. *Our relationship with Creation;*
  3. *Our relationship with each other.*
- Jesus brings peace in all these relationships. Jesus restores this *shalom*.
- The kingdom of heaven is the context in which *shalom* prevails. Things work according to God's original design. Only in this context, true joy is possible.

## QUESTIONS

When have you experienced giving as a delight? When has it not been a joy? Ask God to help you release your grip on worldly riches, so that you can have a servant's heart like Jesus.

## Righteousness

- **Righteousness in the Old Testament** was a relational concept.

  It described a legal relationship. That is, it was a relationship in terms of law, courts, judges, and so on (see Psalm 9:4; Psalm 15; Isaiah 5:7). In other words, it meant ethical or fair behavior.

  It described a covenant relationship. It is a description of God's relating and doing right toward his people; it was also the expected behavior of God's people toward God (see, Ezekiel 18:5–9, 25–32).

- **Righteousness in the New Testament** reflected the two-fold distinction in the Old Testament.

  The Apostle Paul expanded the legal sense of the concept. He applied it to Christ's work. Because of Jesus' atoning death on the cross (he died in our place), God makes right (justifies) sinners (Romans 4:5). Paul did not mean that God makes people righteous—that we can now only do what is right. Rather, he meant that God has applied Christ's righteousness—his perfect obedience and guiltlessness—to us, so we become "legally" (in the sense of a court proceeding) acquitted of the penalty of sin, which is death.

  In Matthew, Jesus was not using the "legal" sense of the concept. Rather, righteousness in the Sermon on the Mount goes back to the "covenant relationship" sense. That is, in the kingdom of heaven, relationships are restored: (1) relationship between God and humanity; (2) relationship between humanity and creation; and (3) relationships among humans. In the kingdom of heaven, people relate rightly, doing what is right in all relationships.

Contributing Authors: William Brent Ashby; Benjamin Galan, MTS, ThM

# Fruit
# of the Spirit

How the Spirit Works
Through Believers

But the fruit of the Spirit is love, joy, peace, patience, kindness, goodness, faithfulness, gentleness and self-control. Against such things there is no law.

–Galatians 5:22, 23

## Good Fruit

• No good tree bears bad fruit, nor does a bad tree bear good fruit. Each tree is recognized by its own fruit. People do not pick figs from thornbushes, or grapes from briers. The good man brings good things out of the good stored up in his heart, and the evil man brings evil things out of the evil stored up in his heart. For out of the overflow of his heart his mouth speaks.

–Luke 6:43-45

• Blessed is the man who does not walk in the counsel of the wicked or stand in the way of sinners or sit in the seat of mockers. But his delight is in the law of the Lord, and on his law he meditates day and night. He is like a tree planted by streams of water, which yields its fruit in season and whose leaf does not wither. Whatever he does prospers.

–Psalm 1:1-3

• The fruit of righteousness will be peace; the effect of righteousness will be quietness and confidence forever.

–Isaiah 32:17

• Make a tree good and its fruit will be good, or make a tree bad and its fruit will be bad, for a tree is recognized by its fruit.

–Matthew 12:33

## Bad Fruit

*Acts of the sinful nature*

| | | |
|---|---|---|
| • sexual immorality | • impurity | • idolatry |
| • debauchery | • factions | • hatred |
| • drunkenness | • jealousy | • lust |
| • filthy language | • witchcraft | • envy |
| • selfish ambition | • orgies | • greed |
| • fits of rage | • slander | • anger |
| • evil desires | • malice | • deceit |

(Galatians 5:19-21; Colossians 3:5-9)

Definition ▷

Jesus' Example ▷

Other Scripture References ▷

Greek Word ▷

# LOVE

## Seeks the highest good of others

**Love** is not based on emotions or feelings. It is a decision to be committed to the well being of others without any conditions or circumstances.

For God so **loved** the world that he gave his one and only Son, that whoever believes in him shall not perish but have eternal life. (John 3:16)

Jesus said: "As the Father has **loved** me, so have I **loved** you. Now remain in my **love**." (John 15:9)

Jesus said, "My command is this: **Love** each other as I have **loved** you. Greater **love** has no one than this, that he lay down his life for his friends. You are my friends if you do what I command." (John 15:12-14)

Dear friends, let us **love** one another, for **love** comes from God. Everyone who **loves** has been born of God and knows God. Whoever does not **love** does not know God, because God is **love**. This is how God showed his **love** among us: He sent his one and only Son into the world that we might live through him. This is **love**: not that we **loved** God, but that he **loved** us and sent his Son as an atoning sacrifice for our sins. Dear friends, since God so **loved** us, we also ought to **love** one another. No one has ever seen God; but if we **love** one another, God lives in us and his **love** is made complete in us. (1 John 4:7-12)

αγαπη: **agape** (pronounced ah-**gah**-pey)

# JOY

## Gladness not based on circumstances

**Definition**

**Joy** is more than happiness. It is not based on financial success, good health, or popularity. By believing in God, obeying his will, receiving his forgiveness, participating in fellowship with other believers, ministering to others, and sharing the Gospel, believers will experience **joy**.

**Jesus' Example**

At that time Jesus, full of **joy** through the Holy Spirit, said, "I praise you, Father, Lord of heaven and earth, because you have hidden these things from the wise and learned, and revealed them to little children. Yes, Father, for this was your good pleasure." (Luke 10:21)

Jesus said: "I am coming to you now, but I say these things while I am still in the world, so that they may have the full measure of my **joy** within them." (John 17:13)

**Scripture**

Jesus said: "Now is your time of grief, but I will see you again and you will **rejoice**, and no one will take away your **joy**. In that day you will no longer ask me anything. I tell you the truth, my Father will give you whatever you ask in my name. Until now you have not asked for anything in my name. Ask and you will receive, and your **joy** will be complete." (John 16:22-24)

Though you have not seen him [Jesus], you love him; and even though you do not see him now, you believe in him and are filled with an inexpressible and glorious **joy**, for you are receiving the goal of your faith, the salvation of your souls. (1 Peter 1:8, 9)

**Greek**

χαρα: **chara** (pronounced **kah**-rah)

# PEACE

## Contentment, unity between people

**Peace** is a state of assurance, lack of fear, and sense of contentment. It is fellowship, harmony, and unity between individuals. Peace is freedom from worry, disturbance, and oppressive thoughts.

For to us a child is born, to us a son is given, and the government will be on his shoulders. And he will be called Wonderful Counselor, Mighty God, Everlasting Father, Prince of **Peace**.
Of the increase of his government and **peace** there will be no end.
He will reign on David's throne and over his kingdom,
establishing and upholding it with justice and righteousness
from that time on and forever. The zeal of the LORD Almighty
will accomplish this. (Isaiah 9:6, 7)

Let us therefore make every effort to do what leads to **peace** and to mutual edification. (Romans 14:19)

For God is not a God of disorder but of **peace**. (1 Corinthians 14:33)

Do not be anxious about anything, but in everything, by prayer and petition, with thanksgiving, present your requests to God. And the **peace** of God, which transcends all understanding, will guard your hearts and your minds in Christ Jesus. (Philippians 4:6, 7)

ειρηνη: **eirene** (pronounced eh-**rey**-ney)

# PATIENCE

## Slow to speak and slow to anger

**Definition**

**Patience** is a slowness in avenging wrongs. It is the quality of restraint that prevents believers from speaking or acting hastily in the face of disagreement, opposition, or persecution. Patience is bearing pain or problems without complaining.

**Jesus' Example**

In a letter to his friend Timothy, the apostle Paul wrote: Here is a trustworthy saying that deserves full acceptance: Christ Jesus came into the world to save sinners—of whom I am the worst. But for that very reason I was shown mercy so that in me, the worst of sinners, Christ Jesus might display his unlimited **patience** as an example for those who would believe on him and receive eternal life. Now to the King eternal, immortal, invisible, the only God, be honor and glory for ever and ever. Amen. (1 Timothy 1:15-17)

**Scripture**

A **patient** man has great understanding, but a quick-tempered man displays folly. (Proverbs 14:29)

A hot-tempered man stirs up dissension, but a **patient** man calms a quarrel. (Proverbs 15:18)

And we urge you, brothers, warn those who are idle, encourage the timid, help the weak, be **patient** with everyone. (1 Thessalonians 5:14)

You too, be **patient** and stand firm, because the Lord's coming is near. Don't grumble against each other, brothers, or you will be judged. (James 5:8, 9)

**Greek**

μακροθυμια: **makrothumia** (pronounced mah-krow-**thew**-me-ah)

# KINDNESS

## Merciful, sweet, and tender

**Kindness** is an eagerness to put others at ease. It is a sweet and attractive temperament that shows friendly regard.

But when the **kindness** and love of God our Savior appeared, he saved us, not because of righteous things we had done, but because of his mercy. He saved us through the washing of rebirth and renewal by the Holy Spirit. (Titus 3:4, 5)

And God raised us up with Christ and seated us with him in the heavenly realms in Christ Jesus, in order that in the coming ages he might show the incomparable riches of his grace, expressed in his **kindness** to us in Christ Jesus. (Ephesians 2:6, 7)

A **kindhearted** woman gains respect, but ruthless men gain only wealth. A **kind** man benefits himself, but a cruel man brings trouble on himself. (Proverbs 11:16, 17)

"Let not the wise man boast of his wisdom or the strong man boast of his strength or the rich man boast of his riches, but let him who boasts boast about this: that he understands and knows me, that I am the LORD, who exercises **kindness**, justice and righteousness on earth, for in these I delight," declares the LORD. (Jeremiah 9:23, 24)

χρηστοτης: **chrestotes** (pronounced krey-**stah**-teys)

# GOODNESS

## Generous and open hearted

**Definition**

**Goodness** is the selfless desire to be open hearted and generous to others above what they deserve.

**Jesus' Example**

But when the kindness and love of God our Savior appeared, he saved us, not because of righteous things we had done, but because of his mercy. He saved us through the washing of rebirth and renewal by the Holy Spirit, whom he poured out on us **generously** through Jesus Christ our Savior, so that, having been justified by his grace, we might become heirs having the hope of eternal life. (Titus 3:4-7)

**Scripture**

Surely **goodness** and love will follow me all the days of my life, and I will dwell in the house of the LORD forever. (Psalm 23:6)

For you were once darkness, but now you are light in the Lord. Live as children of light (for the fruit of the light consists in all **goodness**, righteousness and truth) and find out what pleases the Lord. (Ephesians 5:8-10)

Let us not become weary in doing **good**, for at the proper time we will reap a harvest if we do not give up. Therefore, as we have opportunity, let us do **good** to all people, especially to those who belong to the family of believers. (Galatians 6:9, 10)

**Greek**

αγαθωσυνη: **agathosune** (pronounced ah-**gah**-thow-**soo**-ney)

# FAITHFULNESS

## Dependable, loyal, and full of trust

**Faithfulness** is firm devotion to God, loyalty to friends, and dependability to carry out responsibilities. Faith is the conviction that even now God is working and acting on one's behalf.

Righteousness will be his [Jesus'] belt and **faithfulness** the sash around his waist. (Isaiah 11:5)

When seeing a vision of Jesus, John said: "I saw heaven standing open and there before me was a white horse, whose rider is called **Faithful** and True." (Revelation 19:11a)

But Christ is **faithful** as a son over God's house. And we are his house, if we hold on to our courage and the hope of which we boast. (Hebrews 3:6)

Let love and **faithfulness** never leave you; bind them around your neck, write them on the tablet of your heart. (Proverbs 3:3)

Reprimanding a group of hypocritical religious leaders, Jesus said: "Woe to you, teachers of the law and Pharisees, you hypocrites! You give a tenth of your spices–mint, dill and cummin. But you have neglected the more important matters of the law–justice, mercy and **faithfulness**. You should have practiced the latter, without neglecting the former." (Matthew 23:23)

Be **faithful**, even to the point of death, and I will give you the crown of life. (Revelation 2:10b)

πιστις: **pistis** (pronounced **piss**-tiss)

# GENTLENESS

## Humble, calm, non-threatening

**Definition**

**Gentleness** is a humble non-threatening demeanor that derives from a position of strength and authority, and is useful in calming another's anger. **Gentleness** is not a quality that is weak and passive.

**Jesus' Example**

Jesus said: "Come to me, all you who are weary and burdened, and I will give you rest. Take my yoke upon you and learn from me, for I am **gentle** and **humble** in heart, and you will find rest for your souls. For my yoke is easy and my burden is light." (Matthew 11:28-30)

Matthew quoted Zechariah 9:9 in reference to Jesus' triumphal entry: "Say to the Daughter of Zion, 'See, your king comes to you, **gentle** and riding on a donkey, on a colt, the foal of a donkey.' " (Matthew 21:5)

**Scripture**

A **gentle** answer turns away wrath, but a harsh word stirs up anger. (Proverbs 15:1)

What do you prefer? Shall I come to you with a whip, or in love and with a **gentle** spirit? (1 Corinthians 4:21)

Rejoice in the Lord always. I will say it again: Rejoice! Let your **gentleness** be evident to all. The Lord is near. (Philippians 4:4, 5)

But in your hearts set apart Christ as Lord. Always be prepared to give an answer to everyone who asks you to give the reason for the hope that you have. But do this with **gentleness** and respect. (1 Peter 3:15)

**Greek**

πραυτης: **prautes** (pronounced prah-**oo**-teys)

# SELF-CONTROL

## Behaving well

**Self-control** is to restrain one's emotions, actions, and desires, and to be in harmony with the will of God. Self-control is doing God's will, not living for one's self.

On the night Jesus was betrayed, he knelt down and prayed, "Father, if you are willing, take this cup from me; yet **not my will**, but yours be done." (Luke 22:41, 42)

When they [his accusers] hurled their insults at him [Jesus], he **did not retaliate**; when he suffered, he made no threats. Instead he entrusted himself to him who judges justly. (1 Peter 2:23)

Like a city whose walls are broken down is a man who lacks **self-control**. (Proverbs 25:28)

A fool gives full vent to his anger, but a wise man keeps himself **under control.** (Proverbs 29:11)

For the grace of God that brings salvation has appeared to all men. It teaches us to say "No" to ungodliness and worldly passions, and to live **self-controlled**, upright and godly lives in this present age. (Titus 2:11, 12)

The end of all things is near. Therefore be clear minded and **self-controlled** so that you can pray. (1 Peter 4:7)

εγκρατεια: **egkrateia** (pronounced eg-**krah**-teh-ee-ah)

**But the fruit of the Spirit is love, joy, peace, patience, kindness, goodness, faithfulness, gentleness and self-control. Against such things there is no law.**

**–Galatians 5:22, 23**

# Bearing Fruit

But blessed is the man who trusts in the LORD, whose confidence is in him. He will be like a tree planted by the water that sends out its roots by the stream. It does not fear when heat comes; its leaves are always green. It has no worries in a year of drought and never fails to bear fruit.

–Jeremiah 17:7, 8

For you were once darkness, but now you are light in the Lord. Live as children of light (for the fruit of the light consists in all goodness, righteousness and truth) and find out what pleases the Lord. Have nothing to do with the fruitless deeds of darkness, but rather expose them.

–Ephesians 5:8-11

Remain in me, and I will remain in you. No branch can bear fruit by itself; it must remain in the vine. Neither can you bear fruit unless you remain in me. I am the vine; you are the branches. If a man remains in me and I in him, he will bear much fruit; apart from me you can do nothing.

–John 15:4, 5

Contributors: G. Goldsmith; Shawn Vander Lugt, MDiv; Carol R. Witte

# Armor of God

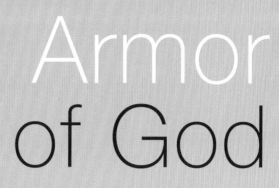

## EPHESIANS 6:10-18

"... Be strong in the Lord and in his mighty power. Put on the full armor of God so that you can take your stand against the devil's schemes."

v. 10-11

The Belt of Truth
The Gospel of Peace
The Shield of Faith
The Breastplate of Righteousness
The Sword of the Spirit
The Helmet of Salvation

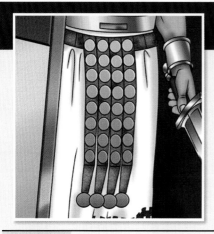

# The Belt of Truth

*With the belt of truth buckled around your waist*
—Ephesians 6:14

| | |
|---|---|
| **Description of Armor** | The "belt of truth" was named after the leather belt with an apron that hung in front of the Roman soldier's groin and lower abdomen. Small brass plates were attached to the apron to provide the greatest possible protection. |
| **Historical Background** | When preparing for battle, the belt would have been the first piece of protective equipment put on by a soldier. It clung closely to the soldier and shielded some of the most vulnerable areas of his body. |
| **Application** | The belt prepares one to be ready for action. Belts were used to tie up the garments so they would not get in the way while fighting. The call to have "your loins girt about with truth" is a call to *be prepared*. Christians always   need to be ready to defend themselves against the powers of darkness and not be caught unaware.<br><br>You can be prepared in every circumstance, by making certain that you are a person of truth. This includes:<br>• Knowing the good news about Jesus and explaining why you believe in him.<br>• Living as a person of integrity—as someone who is honest and trustworthy.<br><br>*Live such good lives . . . that, though they accuse you of doing wrong, they may see your good deeds and glorify God . . .* —1 Peter 2:12 |
| **Other Biblical Passages** | *Always be prepared to give an answer to everyone who asks you to give the reason for the hope that you have. But do this with gentleness and respect . . .* —1 Peter 3:15, 16<br><br>*For God so loved the world that he gave his one and only Son, that whoever believes in him shall not perish but have eternal life.* —John 3:16 |
| **Greek or Latin Term** | *cinculum militaire*—a leather belt |

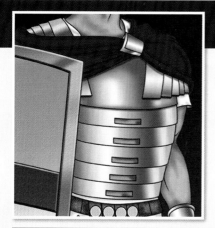

# The Breastplate of Righteousness

*With the breastplate of righteousness in place*
—Ephesians 6:14

The Roman soldier would have fastened the breastplate around his chest.[1] There were two types of breastplates. The first type of breastplate was fashioned by joining several broad, curved metal bands together using leather thongs. The other was a type of chainmail, constructed by linking small metal rings together until they formed a vest.

The purpose of both types of armor was the same—to protect the soldier's vital organs. If a soldier failed to wear his breastplate, an arrow could easily reach a soldier's chest, piercing his heart or lungs.

In Isaiah 59, the LORD puts on "righteousness as a breastplate," and goes to battle against injustice and corruption, restoring peace and order to the land.

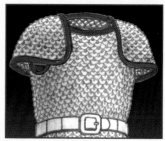

God offers his own righteousness to every believer in Jesus Christ. Righteousness is not something that anyone can gain by doing good deeds. It comes from faith in Jesus Christ. Titus 3:5; Philippians 3:9

Putting on the breastplate of righteousness means:
- Believing in Jesus and his righteousness, not our own. Galatians 2:20, 21

**Breastplate (chainmail)**

- Standing firm against injustice and corruption. Leviticus 19:15, Hebrews 1:9
- Knowing that God promises his protection against the forces of evil for those who have faith in Jesus. 2 Thessalonians 3:3

*[The LORD's] own arm worked salvation for him, and his own righteousness sustained him. He put on righteousness as his breastplate.* —Isaiah 59:16, 17
*For in the gospel a righteousness from God is revealed, a righteousness that is by faith from first to last, just as it is written: "The righteous will live by faith."* —Romans 1:17
*This righteousness from God comes through faith in Jesus Christ to all who believe.* —Romans 3:22

*lorica segmentata*—breastplate with metal bands
*lorica hamata*—chainmail breastplate

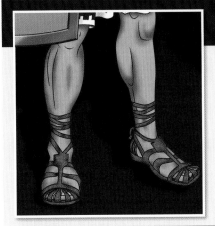

# Feet Prepared with the Gospel of Peace

*And your feet fitted with the readiness that comes from the gospel of peace*

*—Ephesians 6:15*

| | |
|---|---|
| **Description of Armor** | Marching was an essential part of a soldier's life, and no soldier could march far without sturdy shoes. Even before the Roman era, the breaking of a soldier's shoe was a metaphor for weakness or defeat. Isaiah 5:27, 28 The Roman soldier's shoes were fashioned from thick leather and studded through the soles with hobnails.[2] |
| **Historical Background** | The studded soles enabled the soldier to stand firm. They kept the soldier's feet from slipping in battle. Without his shoes, a Roman soldier could not maintain his position against his enemies. |
| **Application** | The Greek word rendered "preparation" or "readiness" in Ephesians 6:15 can also be translated "prepared foundation"—in other words, a firm basis for a soldier's feet.<br><br>The Gospel of Peace is the good news that we can have peace with God. Before we turned to Jesus we wanted to live for ourselves. We did not care about God plans. We were in conflict. But God loves us and made a way of being reconciled with him and living in peace.<br><br>*In Christ we who are many form one body, and each member belongs to all the others.* —Romans 12:5<br><br>The word *peace* has several other uses:<br>• Absence of conflict among Christians. The Lord wants believers to live in peace and unity with one another. 1 Thessalonians 5:13; John 13:35<br>• Absence of worry. This peace is the confidence that God has everything under control. |
| **Other Biblical Passages** | *All this is from God, who reconciled us to himself through Christ and gave us the ministry of reconciliation: that God was reconciling the world to himself in Christ, not counting men's sins against them. And he has committed to us the message of reconciliation.* —2 Corinthians. 5:18, 19<br><br>*Do not be anxious about anything, but in everything, by prayer and petition, with thanksgiving, present your requests to God. And the peace of God, which transcends all understanding, will guard your hearts and your minds in Christ Jesus.* —Philippians 4:6, 7 |
| **Greek or Latin Term** | *caligae*—boot, shoe, sandal<br>*caligati*—"boot men"[3] |

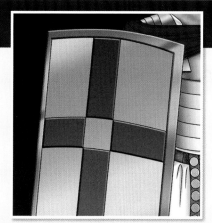

# The Shield
# of Faith

*In addition to all this, take up the shield of faith, with which you can extinguish all the flaming arrows of the evil one.*

—Ephesians 6:16

Made from goat skin or calf skin stretched over sturdy pieces of wood, the Roman shield stood four feet long and was three feet wide. Iron rims were fitted along the top and bottom edges, and an iron circle was attached to the center of the shield. The boards curved inward and a leather strap was fastened to the shield's back.

Before going into battle, Roman soldiers drenched their leather-covered shields with water. When the fiery arrows of their enemies struck these soaked shields, the flames were immediately extinguished.[4] Soldiers could put their shields together and have more protection.

The shield of faith is the Christian's protection against temptation. Whenever we trust that God will provide everything we need, "the spiritual forces of evil" cannot tempt us with the lie that sin can provide a better life than God will. Ephesians 6:12

In this way, "all the flaming arrows of the evil one"— every temptation and distraction that Satan may hurl at God's people—can be stopped. Ephesians 6:16

When faced with authentic faith in God, the powers of darkness are overcome. That is why the apostle John could say, "This is the victory that has overcome the world, even our faith..." 1 John 5:4

*As for God, his way is perfect, He is a shield for all who take refuge in him.*
—2 Samuel 22:31
*My shield is God Most High, who saves the upright in heart.* —Psalm 7:10
*He has prepared his deadly weapons; he makes ready his flaming arrows.* —Psalm 7:13
*You give me your shield of victory, and your right hand sustains me.* —Psalm 18:35
Also Genesis 15:1; Psalm 3:3; 18:2; 28:7; 33:20; 46:9; 76:3

*thyreos*—shield or door
*scutum*—shield

# The Helmet of Salvation

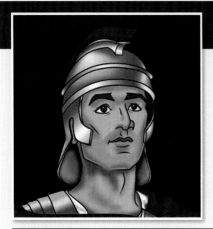

*Take the helmet of salvation*
*—Ephesians 6:17*

| | |
|---|---|
| **Description of Armor** | The Roman soldier's helmet was fashioned from bronze or iron. Two hinged cheek-pieces protected the sides of the soldier's face. For the sake of comfort, soldiers frequently lined their helmets with sponge or felt. At the time of Christ, a crest with a plume of horse's hair was placed on top of Roman helmets. |
| **Historical Background** | The Roman soldier's helmet protected his skull and neck from his enemy's weapons and falling debris. By AD 60, the centurions' plumes were dyed various colors to allow soldiers to distinguish quickly between the rank of different officers.[5] |
| **Application** | The helmet of salvation points to God's ultimate victory over the forces of evil. Jesus' death on the cross and his resurrection from the dead provides all believers with freedom from the bondage of sin, and with eternal life with God in heaven.<br><br>To put on "the helmet of salvation" is to:<br>• Have assurance that Jesus has saved you, not because of good deeds, but because of his mercy. 2 Timothy 1:9<br>• Know that every believer is a "new creation," no longer living for selfish purposes but living for the Lord. 2 Corinthians 5:17<br>• Accept that you are in a battle and will be persecuted for believing in Christ. Keep the faith and you will be blessed. Matthew 5:11, 12<br>• Look forward to being delivered into eternal life. John 3:16<br>• Know that God will forgive his followers when they fall and ask for forgiveness. 1 John 1:9 |
| **Other Biblical Passages** | *[The Lord] put on righteousness as his breastplate, and the helmet of salvation on his head.* —Isaiah 59:17<br>*You also were included in Christ when you heard the word of truth, the gospel of your salvation. Having believed, you were marked in him with a seal, the promised Holy Spirit.* —Ephesians. 1:13<br>*But since we belong to the day, let us be self-controlled, putting on faith and love as a breastplate, and the hope of salvation as a helmet.* — 1 Thessalonians 5:8 |
| **Greek or Latin Term** | *gallic*—helmet<br>*centurion*—Roman military officer who commanded approximately 100 soldiers |

# The Sword
# of the Spirit

*"Take ... the sword of the Spirit, which is the word of God"*
—Ephesians 6:17

The sword of the Roman soldier was a little more than two feet long, and was crafted from iron. Blacksmiths hardened the blade of the sword by covering the red-hot iron with coal dust. The coal dust formed a hard carbon coating on the blade. Sword handles could be made from iron, ivory, bone, or wood.

In battle, rows of Roman soldiers pressed back their enemies one step at a time by forcing their shields forward, using their swords to advance against the enemy. The blade was held flat and parallel to the ground.[6]

The only offensive weapon mentioned in Ephesians 6 is the sword. The belt, breastplate, shoes, shield, and helmet were not offensive; their purpose was defensive, to protect against the enemy. The sword was designed to defeat the enemy's plan and rescue lives. The "word of God" has several meanings:

- **The Gospel,** the message of salvation through Jesus Christ. The Gospel is the good news that Jesus came to save us and give us an abundant life, and life forever with the Lord who loves us. ". . . if you confess with your mouth, 'Jesus is Lord,' and believe in your heart that God raised him from the dead, you will be saved" Romans 10:8-9.

- **The Bible.** When Jesus was tempted by the devil, he used Bible verses to answer and the devil left him. Matthew 4:1-11 Some key verses to memorize when temptations come:
  ✔ God will help you: Isaiah 41:10 ✔ God will always be with you: Joshua 1:9
  ✔ Serve God only: Matthew 4:10 ✔ God helps us when we are tempted: 1 Corinthians 10:13

*And He said to them, "Go into all the world and preach the gospel to all creation.*
—Mark 16:15

*For the word of God is living and active. Sharper than any double-edged sword, it penetrates even to dividing soul and spirit, joints and marrow; it judges the thoughts and attitudes of the heart.* —Hebrews 4:12

*gladius or galdius*—sword

# Background Information

*The description of the Armor of God is found in the New Testament book of Ephesians. Ephesians is a letter written by the Apostle Paul to the followers of Jesus in the city of Ephesus (in Turkey today). The letter was written around AD 60, while Paul was under house arrest in Rome for preaching about Jesus. He was in contact with the Roman palace guards and knew the kind of armor they wore.*

## Who was Paul?

Paul was an apostle of Jesus Christ. As a young man he used to persecute followers of Jesus by having them arrested and jailed. One day, on his way to Damascus, a bright light appeared and blinded him. Jesus spoke to him from heaven and told him to take his message to the Gentiles and the Jews. Paul was converted and baptized. He went on many missionary journeys, and wrote letters to believers in the churches in various cities.

## Life in Ephesus

Ephesus was the center of worship for the goddess Diana (Artemis), and there was a large, famous temple dedicated to her. The area was a major port city of the Roman Empire, and businesses made money by selling silver idols and souvenirs to visitors.

When Paul went there to preach about Jesus, people listened to his message and many became Christians. Some sorcerers who turned to Jesus came together and burned their magic books (worth 50,000 pieces of silver). Local silversmiths and other merchants began to worry that too many people would become Christians, and they started a riot against Paul and his coworkers (Acts 19:17-41).

The riot was put down and a church started in Ephesus. Paul wrote to the new believers about God's love and power. He wanted them to stand firm against the old influences and be devoted to God in love and unity.

## Paul wrote the book of Ephesians from Rome in Italy to the church of Ephesus in Asia

# Stand Firm in Spiritual Warfare

Paul warned the believers in Ephesus that they were in a spiritual battle against unseen forces of darkness. They were struggling against evil powers that were scheming to destroy them. They had to stand firm against the devil and the powers that attack Christians, their families, and their churches. The enemy (the Devil) is clever and tries to attack in many ways—sometimes directly and sometimes in ways that are more subtle (2 Corinthians 11:14, 15).

| Devil's Schemes | God's Plan | Bible |
|---|---|---|
| "Me first" | God first | Matthew 6:33 |
| Lies | Truth | Proverbs 14:25 |
| Fear | Love | 1 John 4:18 |
| Discouragement | Confidence, Strength | Deuteronomy 31:8 |
| Anger | Patience | 2 Timothy 2:24 |
| Condemning others | Putting up with others | Colossians 3:12, 13 |
| Powered by alcohol | Powered by the Holy Spirit | Ephesians 5:18 |
| Complaining | Contentment | Philippians 2:14 |
| "My way" | God's way | Proverbs 16:25 |
| Death | Life | John 5:24 |
| Gossip | Confidentiality | Proverbs 20:19 |
| Regret and shame | God's forgiveness | Acts 3:19 |
| Greed | Giving | Luke 12:15-21 |
| Cursing | Blessing your enemies | Luke 6:28 |
| Revenge | Forgiveness | Matthew 6:14, 15 |
| Hateful talk | Encouragement | Ephesians 4:29 |
| Self-pity | Songs of praise | Ephesians 5:19, 20 |
| Laziness | Productivity, watchfulness | Proverbs 12:24 |
| Unfaithfulness | Loyalty | Philippians 2:4 |
| Irresponsibility | Dependability | Proverbs 14:14 |
| Being rude | Being considerate | Titus 3:2 |
| Worry | Rest | Matthew 11:28, 29 |
| Anxiety | Peace | John 16:33 |
| Jealousy, envy | Abundant heart | James 3:16, 17 |
| Using others | Sacrificing for others | I Corinthians 13:4-7 |
| Rage | Self-control | Colossians 3:8-12 |
| Sexual immorality | Sexual fidelity | 1 Thessalonians 4:3 |
| "My power" | God's power | Ephesians 3:16 |

# Going into Battle

> *Though one person may be overpowered, two can defend themselves. A cord of three strands is not quickly broken.*
> *—Ecclesiastes 4:12*

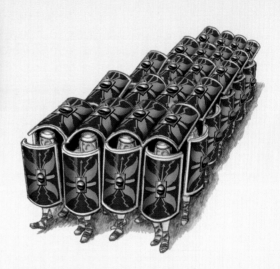

The Roman military worked together using a formation known as "the tortoise." In the tortoise, the rows of soldiers closed all gaps between one another and held their shields at the edges. The first row of men placed their shields in front of them to protect the formation's front; soldiers on the flanks held their shields to the side. The troops in the middle balanced their shields on their helmets and overlapped them, protecting the formation from above.

**Tortoise Formation**

The formation protected the soldiers like a shell protects a tortoise. As long as the soldiers remained together in this formation, they were nearly undefeatable.[7]

It's important to notice that the shield described by Paul was intended to be used in company with others. The rectangular Roman shield was built for use in the tortoise formation. In the same way, our faith is intended to function with other Christians, drawing us together and strengthening us to care for one another. Like Roman soldiers in the tortoise formation, when Christians remain close to each other, they can be strong.

> *Carry each other's burdens, and in this way you will fulfill the law of Christ.*
> *—Galatians 6:2*

References
1. J.B. Campbell, Sr., "Armies, Roman," in Oxford Classical Dictionary 3d ed., ed. Simon Hornblower and Anthony Spawforth (New York: Oxford University Press, 1996) 172-173.
2. Juvenal, *The Satires,* repr., trans. N. Rudd (New York: Oxford University Press, 1999) 16:25.
3. See, for example, Suetonius, "The Deified Augustus," in Lives of the Caesars, trans. C. Edwards (New York: Oxford University Press, 2000) section 25.
4. See Josephus, *The Jewish War,* Books III-IV in Loeb Classical Library (Cambridge, MA: Harvard University Press, 1997) 3:173, where damp ox-hides are placed on palisades for the same purpose.
5. James Yates, *A Dictionary of Greek and Roman Antiquities,* ed. William Smith (London: A. Murray, 1875) 565-66.
6. "Gladius," http://en.wikipedia.org.
7. Craig S. Keener, *The IVP Bible Background Commentary* (Downers Grove, IL: InterVarsity, 1993) 553, 554.

# Personal Prayer

**I am ready to take my stand against the powers of darkness.**

*Please help me to stand against the spiritual forces of evil that want to destroy me, my family, and the church.*

**I buckle the belt of truth around my waist.**

*Help me be a person of truth and reliability. Please give me the words to say when people ask why I follow Jesus. Help me tell about Jesus' death and resurrection and his promise of eternal life to those who believe in him.*

**I take the breastplate of righteousness.**

*Thank you for giving me God's righteousness. Because I am not perfect, God graciously protects me with his own righteousness because I believe in Jesus Christ.*

**I stand firmly on feet prepared with the gospel of peace.**

*Help me to resist temptation and stay away from people, places, and situations that tempt me. Help me live in peace with my family and other believers as much as it depends on me.*

**I lift up the shield of faith.**

*Help me to hold up the shield and stop the arrows of doubt, despair, and hopelessness that the enemy shoots at me.*

**I place upon my head the helmet of salvation.**

*Help me to know that no matter how tough life is, Jesus has conquered sin, and I live with the assurance that I will one day be with God in heaven.*

**I use the sword of the Spirit, the Word of God.**

*Thank you for giving me your Word, the Good News of Jesus Christ. Help me to tell others about him.*

**I will stand guard against the powers of darkness. I will resist temptations and guard myself from vulnerable positions. I will pray persistently for my fellow believers.**

# Ephesians 6:10-18

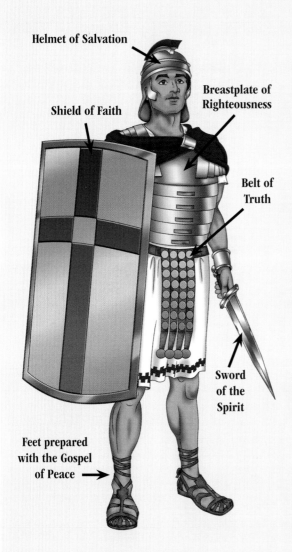

Helmet of Salvation

Breastplate of Righteousness

Shield of Faith

Belt of Truth

Sword of the Spirit

Feet prepared with the Gospel of Peace

10-12: Finally, be strong in the Lord and in his mighty power.

Put on the full armor of God so that you can take your stand against the devil's schemes.

For our struggle is not against flesh and blood, but against the rulers, against the authorities, against the powers of this dark world and against the spiritual forces of evil in the heavenly realms.

13: Therefore put on the full armor of God, so that when the day of evil comes, you may be able to stand your ground, and after you have done everything, to stand.

14-15: Stand firm then, with the **belt of truth** buckled around your waist, with the **breastplate of righteousness** in place, and with your **feet fitted with the readiness that comes from the gospel of peace**.

16: In addition to all this, take up the **shield of faith**, with which you can extinguish all the flaming arrows of the evil one.

17: Take the **helmet of salvation** and the **sword of the Spirit**, which is the word of God.

18: And pray in the Spirit on all occasions with all kinds of prayers and requests. With this in mind, be alert and always keep on praying for all the saints.

Author: Timothy Paul Jones, EdD

# ROSE BIBLE BASICS:

# Names of God
# & Other Bible Studies

A FREE downloadable version of this study guide is available at hendricksonrose.com. Click on "information", click on "Free Study Guide Samples", click on "FREE Rose Bible Basics Study Guides and Worksheets" then click on "Names of God Study Guide".

The leader guide covers each chapter of this book and includes teaching tips, additional resources, and answer keys for the study guide worksheets.
The study guide includes a reproducible worksheet and/or discussion questions for each chapter.

**What participants will gain from this study:**
- Deepen their understanding of God, Jesus, and the Holy Spirit through learning about God's names.
- Be able to correct misunderstandings about the Trinity and to defend the deity of Jesus from Scripture.
- Learn how to apply Jesus' teachings, such as the Beatitudes and the Lord's Prayer, in their daily lives.
- Understand what it means to develop Christian character by studying the Ten Commandments, Fruit of the Spirit, and Armor of God.

# LEADER GUIDE

Spend time in prayer before each study session and pray for each participant.

## CHAPTER 1: NAMES OF GOD

### Main Idea

God's names reveal that he is almighty, eternal, our healer, sanctifier, provider, and much more!

### Teaching Tips

Introduce participants to the purposes of this study. Ask them what they hope
  to gain from the study or why they joined this study.

Choose as many names of God as time permits and use the names in prayer,
  emphasizing their meaning and relevance in our lives. (For example:
  Jehovah-Rapha, the Lord who heals; Pray: "Lord, you bring healing in our
  lives by...")

See the personal reflection and worship suggestions at the end of the chapter
  for more ideas.

### Digging Deeper

For more about the attributes of God use a systematic theology book, and
  bring it to the session to dig deeper into what the Bible teaches about God.
  See *Foundations of the Christian Faith* by James M. Boice (InterVarsity:
  1986) and *Systematic Theology* by Wayne Grudem (Zondervan: 1995).

### Worksheet Key

(1) d   (2) c   (3) True   (4) a   (5) d

## CHAPTER 2: NAMES OF JESUS

### Main Idea

Jesus' names reveal that he is Messiah, God, king, our savior, sustenance,
  light, and much more!

### Teaching Tips

If participants are new believers or seekers, give a brief overview of the life of
  Jesus before covering Jesus' names. Explain why he came and what his
  death and resurrection mean for us today. As you teach, connect these beliefs
  with the names of Jesus.

Choose as many names of Jesus as time permits and use the names in prayer,
  emphasizing their meaning and relevance in our lives. (For example, pray:
  "Lord Jesus, our Bread of Life, you sustain our lives by...")

Taken from Rose Bible Basics: Names of God & Other Bible Studies #663X   ISBN:9781596362031

**Digging Deeper**

For questions and answers about the historicity of Jesus, the Gospels, and
Jesus' death and resurrection, see *Jesus: Fact & Fiction* pamphlet available
at www.rose-publishing.com.

**Worksheet Key**

(1) True   (2) b   (3) d   (4) a   (5) True

# CHAPTER 3: NAMES OF THE HOLY SPIRIT

## Main Idea

The Holy Spirit's names reveal that he is powerful, wise, gracious, our
counselor, life, judge, and much more!

## Teaching Tips

Bring the chapters on the names of God, Jesus, and the Holy Spirit together by
showing how the names portray a triune God. For example, God's name El
Olam means "Eternal God;" Jesus is called "Eternal Father"; the Holy Spirit
is the "Eternal Spirit." Ask participants: Which connections between the
names can you find?

Look through the book of Acts and find examples of the power and
guidance the Holy Spirit provides in the ministry of the first Christians.
Some examples: Acts 2:1–4; 5:1–11; 9:31; 21:10–11.

Also see the study tip under "Gifts of the Holy Spirit" in this chapter.

## Digging Deeper

*Discovering Your Spiritual Gift* by Kenneth Kinghorn (Zondervan: 1984).

## Worksheet Key

(1) False   (2) a   (3) c   (4) False   (5) d

# CHAPTER 4: THE TRINITY

## Main Idea

There is only one God, and this God exists as one essence in three persons:
Father, Son, and Holy Spirit.

## Teaching Tips

The worksheet activity provided for this chapter may take more time than
usual, so plan your session accordingly. This activity can be done at the
beginning or near the end of the session.

## Digging Deeper

For further study, see the resources listed at the end of the chapter.

## Worksheet

If the class is large, break them into three smaller groups. Assign each group a different list of verses from the worksheet. If the class is small, have all participants complete the worksheet together. When the groups complete their portion of the worksheet, list all the attributes and activities they found from the Scriptures onto a whiteboard or easel pad. Ask participants: What similar attributes and activities do you notice across all three: Father, Son, and Holy Spirit? Remember, this activity is not a competition. It encourages participants to interpret Scripture themselves, and to understand how the Bible teaches the doctrine of the Trinity using a variety of passages taken together, rather than just all in one verse.

# CHAPTER 5: THE TEN COMMANDMENTS

## Main Idea

God's commandments teach us to value what God values and to always remember that he is our first priority.

## Teaching Tips

Participants may not be clear about obedience, grace, and salvation in relation to God's commandments. It may be helpful to discuss these issues with the group:

- Does obedience to the Ten Commandments make one a good person?
- Does being good earn or guarantee salvation?
- Is it possible live up to all God's commandments?
- What happens when a believer breaks a commandment? Does he or she lose salvation?

## Digging Deeper

To learn more about specific Old Testament concepts such as Sabbath, idolatry, law, etc., use a Bible dictionary, for example, *Nelson's New Illustrated Bible Dictionary* by Ronald F. Youngblood (Nelson: 1995).

## Worksheet Key

(1) c   (2) e   (3) a   (4) f   (5) g   (6) d   (7) h   (8) b   (9) j   (10) i

# CHAPTER 6: THE LORD'S PRAYER

## Main Idea

God is our holy and loving Father who cares for our needs and the needs of others.

## Teaching Tips

Allow for plenty of time for praying together. Pray by following the seven attributes of God in the seven parts of the Lord's Prayer.

Sing or recite together the Lord's Prayer to open and/or close the session.

Taken from Rose Bible Basics: Names of God & Other Bible Studies #663X   ISBN:9781596362031

## Digging Deeper

For more on prayer, see *Alone with God* by John MacArthur, Jr. (Cook Communications Ministries: 1995). The "How Can I Pray?" section in this chapter is an excerpt from *Alone with God.*

## Worksheet Key

(1) False   (2) d   (3) False   (4) e   (5) e

# CHAPTER 7: THE BEATITUDES

## Main Idea

The Beatitudes are about life in the kingdom of God—a life that Jesus teaches is far better than the way of the world.

## Teaching Tips

Discussion questions are located within the chapter. Because some of the questions are more personal than others, be sure to select questions appropriate for the level of sharing that participants are comfortable with.

## Digging Deeper

Put the Beatitudes in context in the Sermon on the Mount. For an outline and explanation of the Sermon on the Mount, see Bible commentaries, such as *World Biblical Commentary: Matthew 1–13* by Donald A. Hagner (Thomas Nelson Publishers: 1993).

## Worksheet Key

(1) b   (2) False   (3) b   (4) True   (5) c

# CHAPTER 8: FRUIT OF THE SPIRIT

## Main Idea

Believers have been made free in Christ to live, not by the sinful flesh, but by the Spirit.

## Teaching Tips

Have participants read the context of the Fruit of the Spirit: Gal. 5:13–25. Compare and contrast the Fruit of the Spirit with the acts of the sinful nature (flesh).
Explain the background to the book of Galatians to put the Fruit of the Spirit in context:
- Why Paul wrote this letter to the Galatian believers.
- What Paul says about the law and being free in Christ.
- What Paul means by living according to the spirit and not the sinful nature.

## Digging Deeper

For background to the book of Galatians, see *New American Commentary: Galatians* by Timothy George (B&H: 1994).

**Worksheet Key**
(1) d   (2) a   (3) f   (4) c   (5) b   (6) h   (7) e   (8) i   (9) g

## CHAPTER 9: ARMOR OF GOD
**Main Idea**
Putting on the armor of God helps us stand strong against the devil's schemes.

**Teaching Tips**
Have participants break into groups of 3 or 4. Have each group answer the
   following questions using these passages on spiritual warfare:
   Rom. 16:17–20; 2 Cor. 10:3–5; 1 John 4:1–6.
   - What are false teachings and false spirits?
   - How can we resist being deceived?
   - What promises does Scripture give us about this struggle?
At the end of the session, pray the "Personal Prayer" together located at the
   end of this chapter.

**Digging Deeper**
Put the Armor of God in context by using a concise Bible commentary for life
   application and to outline of the book of Ephesians. See *The Message of
   Ephesians* by John Stott (InterVarsity: 1984).

**Worksheet Key**
(1) d   (2) a   (3) b   (4) e   (5) c   (6) f

# FEEDBACK
To improve future studies, be sure to get feedback from the group about
   teaching style, meeting location, discussion time, material covered, length of
   study, and group size. Choose a method that best suits your group:
   Anonymous evaluation sheet, e-mail response or questionnaire, open
   discussion. (See the feedback questions at the end of the study guide.)

*Note: The inclusion of a work or website does not necessarily mean endorsement of all its
   contents or of other works by the same author(s).*

# STUDY GUIDE

The study guide which begins on the following page includes, for each
   chapter, a reproducible worksheet and/or discussion questions for group
   discussion or personal reflection.

# NAMES OF GOD

**Worksheet**

1.  A 16<sup>th</sup> century translator wrote the name YHVH using the vowels of *Adonai* to come up with which name?
    a.  Elohim
    b.  El Shaddai
    c.  Immanuel
    d.  Jehovah

2.  What is the meaning of *El Roi* which Hagar called the Lord beside a fountain of water in the wilderness?
    a.  The God of Israel
    b.  I AM
    c.  The God Who Sees Me
    d.  The Self-Existent One

3.  True of False? *Jehovah-Shalom* means "The Lord is Peace."

4.  What is the meaning of *El Elyon* which Melchizedek called God when he blessed Abram?
    a.  God Most High
    b.  God of the Mountains
    c.  The Lord is my Banner
    d.  The Lord is Peace

5.  What is the meaning of *Jehovah-Nissi* which Moses named the altar he built for God after a victory in battle?
    a.  The Lord our Righteousness
    b.  Creator
    c.  The Eternal God
    d.  The Lord is My Banner

**Discussion Questions**

1.  Which names of God in this chapter stood out to you? And why?
2.  There are many names of God in the Bible. How do so many names help us to relate to God better?
3.  Which names of God are you most comfortable with using in prayer? Which ones do you feel uncomfortable using?
4.  Choose one of the names of God. How have you experienced God reveal himself in that way in your life?

# NAMES OF JESUS

**Worksheet**

1. True or False? The word *Christ* is the Greek translation of *Messiah* which means "anointed one."

2. Which name of Jesus focuses on Jesus as the fulfillment of the sacrificial system and the sacrifice that pays for our sins?
   a. Shiloh
   b. Lamb of God
   c. Emmanuel
   d. All of the above

3. Which name of Jesus focuses on Jesus as the One we rely on?
   a. Bread of Life
   b. True Vine
   c. Chief Cornerstone
   d. All of the above

4. *Jesus*, the Greek word for *Yeshua,* means:
   a. Jehovah is salvation
   b. God with us
   c. Witness
   d. Messenger of the Covenant

5. True or False? Jesus is called *Apostle* in the New Testament?

**Discussion Questions**

1. Which names of Jesus in this chapter stood out to you? And why?
2. What are some similarities you notice between the names of God and the names of Jesus?
3. One of Jesus' titles is *Son of God* and believers are called *sons of God* as well (Gal. 3:26). How is our relationship to God similar to Jesus' and in what ways is it different?
4. Which names of Jesus are you most comfortable with using in prayer? Which ones do you feel uncomfortable using?
5. Choose one of the names of Jesus. How have you experienced Jesus reveal himself in that way in your life?

# NAMES OF THE HOLY SPIRIT

**Worksheet**

1. True or False? The Holy Spirit is an impersonal force emanating from God?

2. Which name of the Holy Spirit focuses on how he cleanses and purifies us from evil?
   a. Spirit of Burning
   b. Comforter
   c. Spirit of Revelation
   d. Spirit of Might

3. Which name of the Holy Spirit focuses on how he leads us and teaches us?
   a. Breath of the Almighty
   b. Spirit of Glory
   c. Spirit of Counsel
   d. Spirit of Life

4. True or False? Only mature believers have the Holy Spirit in them.

5. Which of the following is <u>not</u> part of baptism of the Holy Spirit?
   a. Initiation
   b. Infusion
   c. Identification
   d. Individualism

**Discussion Questions**

1. Which names of Holy Spirit in this chapter stood out to you? And why?
2. What are the similarities you notice between the names of God, names of Jesus, and names of the Holy Spirit?
3. One task of the Holy Spirit is praying along side us (Rom. 8:26–27). What does this look like in your life or in the lives of believers you know?
4. Which names of Holy Spirit are you most comfortable with using in prayer? Which ones do you feel uncomfortable using?
5. Choose one of the names of Holy Spirit. How have you experienced the Holy Spirit reveal himself in that way in your life?

# THE TRINITY

Look up each Scripture passage below and on a separate piece of paper list all the attributes and activities described. (Some are already begun for you.)

## Attributes and Activities of...

### The Father
Psalm 100:3—*Creator. Owner of us. Authority over his creation.*
1 John 3:20      Ps. 138:3         Gen. 1:1         Eph. 1:4–5       Jer. 23:24
Rom. 16:25–27 John 5:21

### The Son
Col. 1:16–17—*All creation through him. Without him nothing could exist.*
John 5:21         Rev. 1:17–18   John 1:4          John 21:17       Phil. 4:13
Eph. 1:22–23    Romans 8:10    Matt. 8:31–32

### The Holy Spirit
1 Cor. 2:10–11—*Knows the deep things of God. Reveals the things of God.*
Heb. 9:14          1 Cor. 12:11                   Eph. 3:16          Ps. 139:7
Ps. 104:30        Rom. 8:11

Compare all three lists. What similar attributes and activities do you notice across all three? What does this tell us about God the Father, the Son, and the Holy Spirit?

## Discussion Questions

1. After reading this chapter, what did you learn about the Trinity that you previously didn't know or misunderstood?
2. Why is Jesus' divinity important for our relationship with God?
3. The three Persons of the Trinity are in relationship with one another. Does God existing in relationship make a difference in how we should live? Why or why not?
4. What are some practical things you can do to help you relate to God as triune—Father, Son, and Holy Spirit?
5. What questions do you still have about the Trinity and would like to learn more about?

# THE TEN COMMANDMENTS

**Worksheet**

Match the things that God does not want in our lives with their opposites.
(Use each only once.)

**God does <u>not</u> want us to ...**

1. _____ Have another god before him

2. _____ Make graven images (idols)

3. _____ Take God's name in vain

4. _____ Forget the Sabbath day

5. _____ Dishonor one's father and mother

6. _____ Kill (murder)

7. _____ Commit adultery

8. _____ Steal

9. _____ Lie

10. _____ Covet

**Instead, God wants us to ...**

a. Revere God as holy

b. Be productive and give generously

c. Give him our first loyalty

d. Hold life as sacred

e. Know that God is bigger than any representation

f. Remember to take time to worship God

g. Respect those in authority

h. Be faithful and pure

i. Be content with what you have

j. Be honest

## Discussion Questions

1. When you hear about the "Ten Commandments" what social issues, images, or ideas today do you associate with it? What might the ancient Israelites associated it with?
2. What happens when a believer today breaks a commandment? Does he or she lose salvation?
3. Jesus said that the greatest commandment is to "love the Lord your God" with all that you are (Matt. 22:37–38). How does love for God affect a person's obedience to God's other commandments?
4. Jesus said the second greatest commandment is to "love your neighbor as yourself" (Matt. 22:39). Who is your "neighbor"?
5. How can or should believers observe the "Sabbath" today?

# THE LORD'S PRAYER

**Worksheet**

1. True or False? Addressing God as "Father" in prayer was a common practice in Jesus' day.

2. To "hallow" God's name means to:
    a. Misuse God's name
    b. Speak God's name
    c. Clear God's name as justified
    d. Honor God's name as sacred

3. True or False? God's kingdom will come in the future, but is <u>not</u> yet here and now.

4. The "debts" referred to in "forgive us our debts" are:
    a. Our sins
    b. Our spiritual debts
    c. Our neglect of doing good
    d. (a) and (b)
    e. All of the above

5. By asking God for "our daily bread" we are:
    a. Acknowledging that our life depends on his mercy
    b. Not taking God's mercy for granted
    c. Asking for physical things we need
    d. (a) and (b)
    e. All of the above

**Discussion Questions**

1. When did you first hear the Lord's Prayer? Did you grow up reciting it? Singing it? Is it new to you?
2. How does addressing God as "Father" in prayer change the way you see God, and the way you see yourself in relation to him?
3. The Lord's Prayer shows us that we need to ask God for our daily bread. What are some "daily breads" in your life that you can ask God for each day?
4. With so many good reasons to forgive, why do you think it is often difficult to forgive? How can you learn to forgive others more?
5. In Matthew 6:14–15 we learn that God will not forgive us if we refuse to forgive others. Is there someone you are holding resentment against?

Taken from Rose Bible Basics: Names of God & Other Bible Studies #663X   ISBN:9781596362031

# THE BEATITUDES

**Worksheet**

1. The Latin word *beatus,* from where we get *beatitude,* means:
   a. Kingdom
   b. Happy
   c. Peace
   d. None of the above

2. True or False? By fulfilling the Beatitudes commandments a person will be allowed to enter the kingdom of heaven.

3. To be "meek" in the Bible means to be:
   a. Passive
   b. Humble
   c. Shy
   d. Proud

4. True or False? Having a pure heart is <u>not</u> the result of personal effort and <u>not</u> something we work toward.

5. When God makes right (justifies) sinners, this means that they:
   a. Can only do what is right.
   b. Are still "legally" guilty of their sin before God.
   c. Have Christ's righteousness applied to them.
   d. Earned their righteousness through practicing the Beatitudes.

*(Discussion questions are located within the chapter.)*

# FRUIT OF THE SPIRIT

**Worksheet**

Match the traits on the left with their descriptions on the right. (Use each only once.)

1. _____ Love
2. _____ Joy
3. _____ Peace
4. _____ Patience
5. _____ Kindness
6. _____ Goodness
7. _____ Faithfulness
8. _____ Gentleness
9. _____ Self-control

a. Gladness not based on circumstances
b. Merciful and tender
c. Bearing pain or problems without complaining
d. Seeks the highest good of others
e. Full of trust
f. Contentment
g. Restraining oneself to be in harmony with God's will
h. Generous and open hearted
i. Humble, calm and non-threatening

**Discussion Questions**

1. Read John 15:4. How do believers remain in Jesus?
2. Is the *Fruit of the Spirit* a list of things we need to do to be saved? If a believer has more "fruit" in their life than another believer can they be more sure they are saved?
3. Read Galatians 3:1–5. In your own words, explain what is being said in this passage?
4. Sometimes gentleness is thought of negatively—being weak and passive. How was Jesus gentle, yet still strong and active in his life and ministry?
5. Why do you think love is so highly esteemed in the Bible? How does love affect the other fruits?

# ARMOR OF GOD

**Worksheet**

Match the Armor of God with their descriptions. (Use each only once.)

1. _____ Belt of Truth

2. _____ Breastplate of Righteousness

3. _____ Feet Prepared with the Gospel of Peace

4. _____ Shield of Faith

5. _____ Helmet of Salvation

6. _____ Sword of the Spirit

a. Firmly against injustice, corruption, and the forces of evil

b. Readiness, prepared foundation, and a firm basis

c. Christ's ultimate victory over death and the forces of evil

d. The first piece of protective equipment put on by a soldier

e. Protection against temptation and Satan's "flaming arrows"

f. An offensive weapon to defeat the enemy's plan and rescue lives

## Discussion Questions

1. What historical background information about Roman armor stood out to you? And why?

2. Read 2 Corinthians 10:3–5. What are some examples in today's world of "arguments" and "pretensions" against the "knowledge of God"? How do believers use the Armor of God against them?

3. In your own words, what does it mean to be a person of truth?

4. What does carrying the "shield of faith" look like in the lives of believers?

5. The "sword of the Spirit" (the word of God) is the only offensive weapon mentioned. How does a believer use the word of God for offense to defeat the devil's schemes?

# FEEDBACK

1. What did you learn through this study that deepened your relationship with God and/or helped you understand biblical teachings better?

   _____

   _____

2. What was your favorite thing about this study, and why?

   _____

   _____

3. How could the meeting location, setting, length, or time be improved?

   _____

   _____

4. Did you think the material covered was too difficult, too easy, or just right? _____

   _____

5. What would you like to see different about the group discussions?

   _____

   _____

6. What would you like to see different about the worksheets?

   _____

   _____

7. What topic would you like to learn more about? _____

   _____

# Other Rose Publishing Books

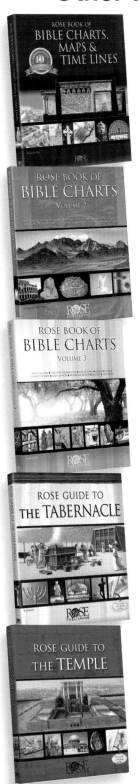

### Rose Book of Bible Charts, Maps & Time Lines

A must-have resource for every pastor, teacher, and Bible study leader for the past ten years. Now get the updated and redesigned Anniversary Edition of this best-selling book, *Rose Book of Bible Charts, Maps and Time Lines 10th Anniversary Edition*!

Enjoy this best-selling book expanded with new charts, upgraded maps highlighting modern-day cities and countries, and up-to-date facts and statistics! Includes 216 reproducible pages of illustrations, charts, and maps on a variety of Bible topics, with two fold-outs of the genealogy of Jesus, a cutaway tabernacle illustration, and a Bible time line.
Hardcover. 230 pages. ISBN: 9781596360228

### Rose Book of Bible Charts, Volume 2

Topics include: Bible Translations comparison chart • Why Trust the Bible • Heroes of the Old Testament • Women of the Bible • Life of Paul • Christ in the Old Testament • Christ in the Passover • Names of Jesus • Beatitudes • Lord's Prayer • Where to Find Favorite Bible Verses • Christianity and Eastern Religions • Worldviews Comparison • 10 Q & A on Mormonism/Jehovah's Witnesses/Magic/Atheism and many others!
Hardcover. 240 pages. ISBN: 9781596362758

### Rose Book of Bible Charts, Volume 3

Topics include: Who I Am in Christ (Assurance of Salvation) • What the Bible Says about Forgiveness • What the Bible Says about Money • What the Bible Says about Prayer • Spiritual Disciplines • Heaven • Attributes of God • How to Explain the Gospel • Parables of Jesus • Bible Character Studies and many more!
Hardcover. 240 pages. ISBN: 9781596368699

### Rose Guide to the Tabernacle

Full color with clear overlays and reproducible pages. The tabernacle was the place where the Israelites worshiped God after the exodus. Learn how the sacrifices, utensils, and even the structure of the tabernacle were designed to show us something about God. See the parallels between the Old Testament sacrifices and priests' duties, and Jesus' service as the perfect sacrifice and perfect high priest. See how: The Tabernacle was built • The sacrifices pointed to Jesus Christ • The design of the tent revealed God's holiness and humanity's need for God • The ark of the covenant was at the center of worship.
Hardcover. 128 pages. ISBN: 9781596362765

### Rose Guide to the Temple

Simply the best book on the temple in Jerusalem. It is the only full-color book from a Christian viewpoint that has clear plastic overlays showing the interior and exterior of Solomon's Temple, Herod's Temple, and the Tabernacle. Contains more than 100 color diagrams, photos, illustrations, maps, and time lines of more than 100 key events from the time of King David to modern day. It also includes two full-color posters: the temple of Jesus' time and the stunning National Geographic poster on the Temple Mount through time. You will understand how the temple looked, its history, and its biblical importance.
Hardcover. 144 pages. ISBN: 9781596364684

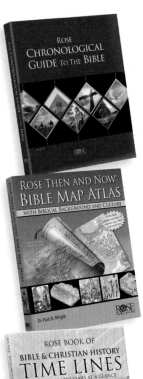

## Rose Chronological Guide to the Bible

Look at the Bible in a fresh new way by viewing Bible events in the order they happened. This one-of-a-kind resource is packed with full-color charts, maps, and illustrations to help you explore Bible history. It includes:

- Three 24-inch chronology foldouts showing the Bible at a glance, the life of Jesus, and the kings and prophets of the Old Testament.
- Chronology charts on popular Bible topics such as the Genesis flood, the temple in Jerusalem, the ark of the covenant, and more.
- A harmony of the four Gospels—Matthew, Mark, Luke, and John—side by side.
- Maps showing the journeys of the patriarchs, the exodus route, where Jesus walked, Paul's missionary trips, and more.

Hardcover. 182 pages. ISBN: 9781628628074

## Rose Then and Now® Bible Map Atlas
### with Biblical Background and Culture

Your 30 favorite Bible characters come alive with this new Bible atlas. Find out how the geography of Bible lands affected the culture and decisions of people such as David, Abraham, Moses, Esther, Deborah, Jonah, Jesus, and the disciples.
Hardcover. 272 pages. ISBN: 9781596365346

## Rose Book of Bible & Christian History Time Lines

Six thousand years and 20 feet of time lines in one hard-bound cover! These gorgeous time lines printed on heavy chart paper can also be slipped out of their binding and posted in a hallway or large room for full effect. The Bible Time Line compares scriptural events with world history and Middle East history. Shows hundreds of facts; includes dates of kings, prophets, battles, and key events. The Christian History Time Line begins with the life of Jesus and continues to the present day. Includes key people and events that all Christians should know.
Hardcover. ISBN: 9781596360846

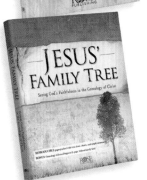

## Jesus' Family Tree

Packed with time lines, family trees, and simple summaries, this incredible reference book gives a fantastic overview of 30 key people in Jesus' ancestry. The remarkable heroes and heroines in the ancestry of Jesus teach us a lot about God's faithfulness over the centuries. Each character in Jesus' family tree gives us a glimpse of how God works all things—even the tragedies and missteps—together for good.
Hardcover. 192 pages. ISBN: 9781628620085

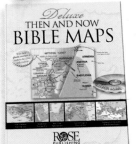

## Deluxe Then and Now® Bible Maps
### Book with CD-ROM!

See where Bible places are today with Then and Now® Bible maps with clear plastic overlays of modern cities and countries. This deluxe edition comes with a CD-ROM that gives you a JPG of each map to use in your own Bible material as well as PDFs of each map and overlay to create your own handouts or overhead transparencies. PowerPoint® fans can create their own presentations with these digitized maps.
Hardcover. 40 pages. ISBN: 9781596361638